Curtain Up

Curtain Up

Dave Hopwood

The National Society
*Leading Education
with a Christian Purpose*
Church House Publishing

National Society/Church House Publishing
Church House
Great Smith Street
London SW1P 3NZ

ISBN 0 7151 4933 4

Published 2000 by the National Society (Church of England) for Promoting Religious Education and Church House Publishing.

Cover design by Leigh Hurlock
Printed in England by The Cromwell Press Ltd, Trowbridge, Wiltshire

Contents

Introduction

The Bible is the biggest seller of all time. I'm sure you probably knew that. It's an amazing book, at times awe-inspiring, faith-inducing and life-changing. Yet at other times it can appear to be the most difficult read in the world. There are days when we can't put it down and, equally, days when we can't pick it up.

Personally speaking, I love the Bible, I love the stories, the insights, the creativity, the honesty and the real people emblazoned across its pages. Yet as I write this I'm conscious that I haven't picked mine up and read it properly for a week. Ironic, isn't it?

That's one of the reasons for this book. All the sketches wedged between these pages are based on stories from the Bible. They are not of course intended in any way to be a replacement for reading it, simply a vehicle for bringing a few of the stories to life in a way that may appeal to children of all ages.

We mustn't forget, of course, that when most of the Bible stories actually took place they were seen and experienced, not read on the printed page. They were, as Paul puts it, living letters from God, so they were visual, they were active, and they incorporated sounds, sweat and smells. That's what made them memorable. It's hard to argue with a man born blind when he's standing in front of you counting your freckles for the first time.

This is one of the things I love about the Bible – as you begin to delve into these stories, as you put yourself in the picture, you discover more and more about who God is, the way he works, and the frail feeble people he chooses for his friends – people like you and me.

So, as you read these scripts, as you prepare them, rehearse and rehash them, I hope that it takes you back to the original and to the stories that turned a world upside down: stories like that of Christmas, so familiar to us of course, but what a risk! Have you ever considered how many babies probably died on that same night that Jesus was born in the dirt and the squalor? Or consider Easter, another familiar tale, yet so steeped in drama it cries out to be lifted from the printed page and retold in song, mime, drama, rap, verse, puppetry or dance . . . Then there are the tales of the rogues that Jesus chose to be his best friends: Mean Matthew and Pilfering Zac, to name just two. And of course there are also the tales that Jesus himself told to illustrate a vibrant new world no one had yet imagined.

So, when you embark upon the telling of these tales, give it your best shot. To help you do just that, here are four quick tips:

1.   Give 100 per cent. Don't hold back but throw yourself in totally, even if it does feel like the deep end sometimes!

2.   Make time for proper preparation. If you're doing the piece in a service or event it may well communicate more than the sermon, so take time to get it up to speed.

3.   Be encouraging and be kindly critical. Appoint a director who can ensure the piece looks and sounds good. Pat each other on the back and point out the bits that need a little tweaking.

4.   Pray . . . and enjoy it! This is easier said than done when your principal character has gone down with flu and the vicar has changed his sermon at the last minute, but God wants you to succeed far more than you do, so, even if it feels like a failure, pray, commit it to him, give every ounce of energy and let him use your weakness to communicate his perfect strength.

God has given us some great stories. Let's tell them with confidence, good humour and humility.

Go for it!

Christmas

The snowman

Bible references
Luke 2.1-20

Themes
Christmas, the story of the baby in the stable and the innkeeper

Cast
Snowman
Boy
Innkeeper
Shepherd

Props
Some sort of white, round costume for the Snowman,
with hat, pipe, etc., Crook and hat for the Shepherd

The scene begins in the Boy's bedroom. He is playing with a model aeroplane. He walks to the window and looks out. While he is looking, he rubs his hands and shivers. Behind him the Snowman enters and watches him. Suddenly the Boy turns and runs with his plane. He smashes into the Snowman and they both tumble over.

Boy	Oof! (*Sits up*)
Snowman	Hello!
Boy	Who are you? What are you doing in my bedroom?
Snowman	(*Getting up*) I've come to see you. To say Happy Christmas.
Boy	Well, I'm not happy. I'm cold. And I've got stomach-ache from all that chocolate. And I didn't get the

	present I wanted. And my sister got more than me. And worst of all . . . I had to go to church!
Snowman	Oh! Christmas can be tough, can't it?
Boy	Tough! It's impossible.
Snowman	Hmm. (*He walks to the window and looks out*) Ever thought about the first Christmas?
Boy	(*Looks perplexed*) Umm, not really. It was before I was born. Mary and Joseph had this baby, and there was no room at the inn so they put him in the bulrushes, and King Solomon came and visited him 'cause he was the oldest man that ever lived. And Adam and Eve were his grandparents. Or were they his cousins? Anyway, he had these disciples called Matthew, Mark, Luke and John, and they all wrote books about him and became famous.
Snowman	(*Looks at him*) Do you like adventures?
Boy	(*Grinning*) I like *Bill and Ted's Excellent Adventure*.
Snowman	(*Looks at him*) Do you like journeys?
Boy	(*Grinning*) I like *Bill and Ted's Bogus Journey*.
Snowman	Come on. (*He reaches out a hand.*)
Boy	Where are we going?
Snowman	To Christmas – the first one. Take hold and we'll get there.

(*The Boy slowly walks over and reaches out. As soon as they connect the Boy looks round in amazement, he lets go and starts looking all over.*)

Boy	Wow! How did you do that? Where are we?
Snowman	This – is an inn. A hotel.
Boy	What a dump!

(*The Snowman and Boy are bowled over by a running figure. All collapse on floor.*)

Snowman	Oof! Who are you?

4

Innkeeper	Never mind that! Get out of my way! This is the busiest night in town you know.
Boy	Well, that's because it's Christmas.
Innkeeper	WHAT? What on earth is Christmas?
Boy	Well . . .
Innkeeper	Oh don't bother, I haven't got the time. I've got to put me prices up!
Snowman	That's not very nice.
Innkeeper	Nice! Nice! I'm an innkeeper not Jimmy Saville! I've got a living to make and there's a crowd out there waiting to be ripped o . . . I mean, looking for a place to stay.
Snowman	What's all the fuss about?
Innkeeper	Don't you know? They're taking a census, mate. Roll call, they want to register everyone in the country. You'd better sign up yourself.
Snowman	Hardly – I'm a snowman.
Innkeeper	A what? What's a snowman?
Snowman	(*Looking at the boy*) This is the Middle East, ya know!
Innkeeper	Oof!

(*The Innkeeper is knocked over by another running figure, and all of them end up on the floor again.*)

Snowman	Not again!
Boy	Who are you?
Innkeeper	Never mind that! What sort of room do you want? Pricey, expensive or extortionate?
Shepherd	I don't want a room. I'm looking for the baby.
Boy	Baby? (*He looks at the Snowman, who nods knowingly.*)
Innkeeper	Oh, *them.* They're in the shed.
Snowman and Boy	WHAT!

Innkeeper	What's wrong with you? They're only a couple of peasants.
Snowman	But she has a new baby.
Innkeeper	Yes – and no money. Anyway, how do you know? Are you a relative or something?
Boy	No! He's a snowman.
Innkeeper and Shepherd	A what?
Boy	(*Pointing off stage*) Look!

(*They all duck, hands covering head.*)

Boy	No . . . look.
Innkeeper	(*With distaste*) Oh them!

(*The Boy looks at him, then stamps on his foot.*)

Innkeeper	Ow! You little bu . . . (*He looks round and thinks again*) . . . boy!
Snowman	(*To Shepherd*) That's the people you're looking for.
Shepherd	They've got the baby? Oh! Oh yea . . . oh . . . (*Going all gooey*) Look, look . . . look at him . . . ohh . . .

(*They all crane forward as a group.*)

Innkeeper	Oh . . . isn't she gorgeous!
Boy	He. It's a boy!
Innkeeper	You can tell that from here?
Snowman	We've come a long way to see this baby – we're pretty sure it's a boy.
Shepherd	Blimey! My sheep! I forgot. I hope they're all right!
Boy	(*Pointing to Shepherd's feet*) Ugh! What have you stepped in?
Innkeeper	(*Sniffing*) Phaw, it does smell a bit strong round here.
Snowman	That's the shed, not his feet! Look at it, it's filthy. How could you let her have a baby out there?

6

Shepherd	Yeah, especially a baby like him. Them angels went on and on and on about him. We couldn't shut 'em up.

(They all peer round slowly and stare at the Shepherd.)

Snowman	*(With disbelief)* Angels?
Innkeeper	*(Mocking)* Angels!
Boy	*(Amazed)* Wow! Angels! With wings? *(He flies round like a dive bomber.)*
Shepherd	Shh! You'll wake the baby! Yes, angels. Millions of 'em, all in the sky singing about him. *(Points)* Peace on earth, goodwill to everyone. Apparently this is one important baby.
Innkeeper	Nah. Two weeks' time no one'll ever have heard of him.
Snowman	*(Emphatically)* WRONG!

(They all look at him.)

Snowman	Two thousand years from now, millions of people will remember this day.
Boy	Yes, and Christmas will start in October – according to the supermarkets, anyway.
Innkeeper	What's Christmas?
Shepherd	What's a supermarket?
Boy	Well . . .
Innkeeper	Don't bother – I've got a busy night ahead. I'm off.
Shepherd	Me too – before the sheep get out and leave a trail of whoopsies down the High Street. *(They both leave.)*
Boy	But wait . . . you can't leave the baby in there . . . *(He watches them go, then turns back to the Snowman.)* Will the baby be all right? Will he survive in that stable?
Snowman	Oh yes, he'll live. 'Till later on.
Boy	What do you mean – later on?
Snowman	Come on, I have to go. My time is up. I'm starting to melt.

Boy	NO! You can't! And we can't leave. What's going to happen to the baby?
Snowman	Soon I'll be very slushy, I'm gonna melt and you'll get very wet.
Boy	But the baby . . .
Snowman	(*He keeps walking*) Well . . . yes. He will die too. When he's about 33 . . .
Boy	NO! (*He runs at the snowman and wraps his arms round him tightly.*) NO!
Snowman	(*He laughs kindly*) Yes! It has to be like that. But don't worry, I'll be back – and so will the baby . . . come on, my kneecaps are dripping.

(*They walk off together; the Snowman has his arm around the Boy.*)

A very unstable beginning

Bible references
Luke 2.1-20

Themes
Christmas, the story of the baby, God helping us

Cast
Narrator

Group of four to eight people

Props
None

A group of four to eight mime to the narrative. They begin standing in a line with their backs to the audience.

Narrator: Every day, all over the world, lots of new babies are born.
(All turn and cry.)
　　　　Some are born in royal palaces,
(Look dignified, mime putting on crowns and then suck thumbs.)
　　　　Some are born in the back of a taxi,
(The line leans one way then the other as they make car noises.)
　　　　Some are born in an ambulance,
(Make the sounds of an ambulance siren.)

Some are born in houses,

(*In twos make the shape of a house, using arms to make a pointed roof.*)

And lots are born in hospital.

(*All smile and mime holding babies happily.*)

But not many are born in a stable.

(*Make sounds of cows mooing and lambs bleating.*)

New babies have to be well looked after.

(*Suck thumbs, wail loudly and then nod.*)

They must be clean,

(*Mime washing under arms.*)

Warm,

(*Fan faces and look as if hot.*)

Well fed,

(*Rub stomachs, one person might like to burp. Caution about this!*)

Snug and cosy.

(*All bunch together in a happy cosy group.*)

No one would ever plan to have their baby somewhere where it's cold,

(*All shiver.*)

Dark,

(*All narrow eyes and stick hands out in front as if feeling way forward.*)

Smelly,

(*Sniff and say 'Pooh!'.*)

Dirty;

(*Dust hands off.*)

Full of cobwebs,

(*Mime wiping cobwebs off each other.*)

Rats,

(*Squeak and hold up hands as if they are paws.*)

And insects . . .

(*Scratch and shudder.*)

. . . And germs!

(*All sneeze very loudly at the same time.*)

That would be very dangerous.

(*Say 'Oh oh!' and look round, looking frightened.*)

A newborn baby would not like it and it might even get very ill.

(*All look very worried.*)

No one would plan that, no one except . . . God.

(*Look amazed.*)

His baby was born in a stable where it was very cold,

(*All shiver.*)

Dark,

(*All narrow eyes and stick hands out in front as if feeling way forward.*)

Smelly,

(*Sniff and say 'Pooh!'.*)

Dirty;

(*Dust hands off.*)

Full of cobwebs,

(*Mime wiping cobwebs off each other.*)

Rats,

(*Squeak and hold up hands as if they are paws.*)

And insects . . .

(*Scratch and shudder.*)

. . . And germs!

(*All sneeze very loudly at the same time.*)

He decided his baby would be born like that so he would know what it's like to be poor,

(*Pull out pockets.*)

To be alone,

(All step away from each other and look sad.)

To be cold and frightened.

(Shiver and shudder.)

So he can help us . . . when we feel the same way.

(All step back together as one group and hug each other and freeze.)

Christmas is a time for . . .

by S. Whitfield and R. Browne

Bible reference
Luke 2.1-20

Themes
An introduction to the Christmas story, and to the character of Jesus

Cast
Narrator

Group of two, three or four actors

Props
None

The group illustrates the narration with the actions, sounds and mimed pictures described in italics.

Narrator   Christmas is a time for fun!

(All leap in the air.)

Christmas is a time for games.

(Play leap frog.)

It's a time for friends,

(Huddle together and hug.)

And laughter.

(Laugh.)

There are presents

(*Mime opening presents.*)

And food

(*Eat.*)

Crackers

(*Pull crackers, shout 'BANG'.*)

And carols.

(*Sing 'Away in a manger . . .'.*)

But Christmas doesn't just happen;

(*Panic, shout: 'Agghh!'.*)

We have to prepare.

(*Rush around madly.*)

We have to give a great deal of ourselves

(*Pull out pockets and hold out hands.*)

And our time.

(*Make the shape of a clock.*)

But what's it all about?

(*Shrug.*)

Christmas started a long time ago . . .

(*Turn and look backwards.*)

Before we were born.

(*One person hold a baby.*)

It began with a baby called Jesus.

(*All gather round.*)

When he was born, there were angels singing in the sky,

(*Look up shocked.*)

And people brought him presents.

(*Offer mimed gifts, big and small.*)

And as he grew up he talked to people,

(*Chat together.*)

He laughed with them,

(*Laugh.*)

And cried with them.

(*Cry.*)

He lived his whole life for other people.

(*Hold out hands to audience.*)

And then he died for them too.

(*Form a crucifixion pose, one person being nailed up.*)

Let us introduce you to the best thing about Christmas –

(*One person holds the baby again.*)

Jesus Christ, the Son of God.

(*Others motion towards the baby while looking at the audience.*)

The camel rap

Bible references
Matthew 2.1-12

Themes
The wise men at Christmas

Cast
Narrator
Group of four

Props
Sunglasses for each actor in the group

The group illustrate the sketch with the instructions in italics.
The group are quite rebellious, rather like teenagers, and the Narrator resembles a teacher struggling to keep control.

Narrator   Once there was a camel

(All say: 'Brrr!' and do camel impressions.)

Who was into rapping.

(Group put on sunglasses and rap: 'Hey! Hey! Hey! Hey! Do the camel rap! Do the camel rap! Hey! Hey! Hey! Hey! Do the camel rap! Brrr!')

His name was Kevin.

('KEV - IN!' They chant this.)

Kevin the camel.

('KEV - IN - THE - CAM - EL!')

Yes, yes, all right. *(To the group)* Now Kevin was . . .

(*'KEV - IN - THE - CAM - EL!'*)

      (*Narrator sighs*) Now Kevin . . .

(*'KEV - I . . .' They stop as the Narrator gives them a withering look.*)

      Now Kevin was way ahead of his time – because in those days there was no rapping.

(*'Hey! Hey! . . . Hey? No rapping?'*)

      No rapping.

(*'Ahh!' They all adopt fed-up childish poses.*)

      And camels weren't cool.

(*'Ohh!' They pull off sunglasses and dispose of them, mutter: ''s not fair!', 'I don't wanna do this anymore', 'It's boring', etc . Group turn their backs to the audience and slouch on each other in a fixed pose.*)

      But camels did have the hump . . .

(*'You can say that again!'*)

      So that people could sit on them!

(*Group pose of all sitting on each other.*)

      Especially people who were kings.

(*'What? Rappin' kings? Hey! Hey! Hey! Hey! Do the camel rap!'*)

      No, no, no. Nobody rapped in those days. Instead, kings went on long journeys – to visit babies.

(*Group hold babies in arms.*)

      And this king travelled for two years, with two other kings, and two other camels just to find one baby. In a stable – wrapped in a . . .

(*Wrapped? Hey! Hey! Hey! . . .'*)

      Shh! Or you'll wake the baby.

(*'Where?'*)

      Behind you!

(*Group turn to look at imaginary baby; say 'Ah!' to audience; look again and say 'Ah!' a second time.*)

And this baby was wrapped in an old cloth, inside an old stable

(*Group sniff loudly and say 'Phaw!'*)

Even though he was a new king.

(*'Another king!'*)

Yes – but the most important one of all.

(*'Really?'*)

Yes, 'cause one day

(*Group take one step towards Narrator. 'Yeah?'*)

This king

(*'Yeah?' Group take one step towards Narrator.*)

Will be running things

(*'Yeah?' Group take one step towards Narrator.*)

Forever.

(*'Wow! Amazing . . .' Walk off talking excitedly.*)

Jesus and Easter

Who am I?

Bible reference
Matthew 16.13-20

Themes
Peter's declaration about who Jesus is

Cast
1
2
3
4

Props
Chair

This sketch is led by the group of four, who deliver the narrative in quick-fire succession. Each picture the group make should be frozen while the next piece of narrative is delivered and then the group move into the next scene. A chair is included and should be used in most of the pictures. This is simply to add variety and different levels to the pictures. Feel free to add any other pictures, or to change the suggested ones. The group pictures are outlined in italic type.

1, 2, 3 and 4 begin huddled in a group facing away from the audience, as if watching a television together. 2 turns head and addresses the audience.

2   One day Jesus turned to the people following him and asked them a question:

(All jump round and say together: 'Who do you think I am?')

2   Someone said:

1   'Superman!'

(2 leaps on a chair arms up and others gasp and say – 'Is it a bird? Is it a plane?')

3   Someone else said: 'A right clever Trevor!'

(1 stands on the chair and says in a posh voice, 'Now listen here chaps – I think I just might have all the answers'.)

4   Or . . . 'A good teacher'.

(3 shouts, 'Right you lot – siddownandshuttupp! Or you'll all get 50,000 lines!' Others cower on the one chair.)

1   'A miracle worker'.

(4 leaps on the chair and says, 'Nothing up my sleeves. At no point will my hand leave my wrist. Just like that!')

2   'A salesman'.

(1 knocks on a door, others all answer it, 'Yes?' 1 says, 'Can I interest you in some double glazing?' Others, with big smiles, 'Goodbye!' Slam door.)

3   'A cool dude!'

(2 steps forward and does a Fonzie 'Hey!' Others look amazed and impressed. Any girls in the group swoon.)

4   'A good mate'.

(All argue, 'Shuttup you pratt', 'I hate you', 'Get stuffed!', etc.)

1   'A politician'.

(3 says 'Rhubarb rhubarb rhubarb', possibly as John Major/Maggie Thatcher/Tony Blair. The others sleep.)

2   'A fool'.

(All pose in whacky freezes. Use the chair in this.)

3   'A spaceman'.

(1 says 'A small step for man, but a huge . . . amount of money on the national debt!' All float as if in space, lift up chair to make it look as if this floats too.)

4   'Misguided'.

(2 looks confused 'Er – who am I? What am I doing here? I think I'd like to be a tree.' Others look horrified.)

3   'Just any old bloke'.

(All sniff loudly, laugh, talk. Comments like: 'Whatcha, guv'.)

1   'The Son of God'.

(Others, 'What?' They turn and stare at 1. 2 sits on chair amazed.)

1   'The Son of God'.

(Others, incredulous: 'What?' 1 creeps over and grabs 2's ear and shouts, 'I think he's the Son of God!' All freeze, 2 recoiling.)

Ghost story

Bible references
Matthew 28.1-10, John 20.1-18

Themes
Easter, Resurrection

Cast
Story-teller

Props
None

A responsive story. Teach the audience the key words below, and whenever they hear them during the telling of the story they must respond with the appropriate sound or action.

KEY WORDS:

Rustling – *make a rustling noise*

Whispering – *'whisper, whisper, whisper!'*

Dark – *look scared and wrap your arms around yourself*

Ghost/ghostly – *say 'Wooooooo!' and hold up hands and waggle fingers*

Howling – *all howl*

Dead – *say 'Haaa!' as if shocked*

Vampire – *stick teeth out*

Mummy – *stick arms out front, like in the horror films*

Story-teller   There's an old, old story that took place a long time ago in a graveyard, very early one morning. The place was all **dark**, and all you could hear was the **rustling** of bushes, the **whispering** of the wind as it blew around, and the **howling** of wolves in the distance. The graveyard was all **dark**, with **ghostly** shadows on the pathways and the walls. No one would have dared to go up there that morning, not while it was **dark**, because in that **ghostly** place, with the wolves **howling**, there was a **dead** body lying in there.

However, one person did go that day, one person summoned up the courage to go through the **whispering** wind, and the **rustling** bushes, one person went walking through that **dark** place, and she went there all on her own. And she went there for one reason – to search for the **dead** body.

As she got nearer and nearer, the **whispering** wind grew louder, the **howling** wolves grew louder, and even the **ghostly** shadows grew louder – somehow! But she still went on, nearer and nearer, closer, and closer, step by step by step. Then suddenly, she heard someone behind her, and she felt a hand on her shoulder, and she held her breath. Was it a **vampire**? Was it a **ghost**? Or even worse – an Egyptian **mummy**?

Slowly, very slowly, she turned around and looked. It was still very **dark**, but through the **ghostly** shadows she could just see someone standing there. It wasn't a **ghost**, it wasn't a **vampire**, it wasn't a **mummy**. It was the **dead** man! And he'd come back to see her!

Her mouth fell open, her eyes grew wide with amazement. Then the man spoke, and instantly she knew, he wasn't **dead** any more, and he wasn't a **ghost**, he was alive again, and his name was Jesus, and he'd come back to help her and to help us all with our fears and with all our **darkness**.

The stranger

Bible reference

John 18-21

Themes

An allegory about the life, death and resurrection of Jesus

Cast

Narrator

Group of four to eight who mime the story accompanying the narrative

Props

None

Narrator   The lights were low, the folks were high,

(Shield eyes and squint, punch the air.)

The sun was going down.

(Watch the sun fall stage right.)

The day had passed, the night drew nigh

(All yawn and stretch.)

When trouble hit the town.

(Suddenly look worried.)

The stakes were high in the Blue Saloon

(Mime playing cards.)

When he strode through the door.

(Look stage left suddenly.)

The piana barked out a cowboy croon

(*All play piano.*)

The saloon girls paced the floor.

(*Mime swinging handbags and looking bored.*)

The folks just stopped and stared at him

(*Turn and look stage left again.*)

This stranger dressed in white.

(*Look down at the floor then slowly up.*)

The poker ceased, the lights grew dim

(*Throw down cards.*)

When he stepped in from the night.

(*Lean back from the waist looking wide-eyed and scared.*)

Though he himself, he had no horse,

(*Shrug.*)

No bullets for his gun.

(*Draw guns.*)

He bore the scars of a thousand wars

(*Place hands on chest, as if wounded.*)

Of gunfights lost and won.

(*Turn in twos and draw guns against each other.*)

Well, he hung around while the whisky flowed,

(*All tip back drinks.*)

He mingled with the crowd.

(*All bunch together as a crowd.*)

Folks listened hard to the tales he told

(Place hands to ears.)
>   In a voice both clear and loud.
(Nod slowly and look at each other.)

>   He told them there's much more to life
(Look surprised.)
>   Than girls and fights and bars.
(Freeze about to punch each other.)
>   'Cause this guy said, 'When your carcass is dead,
(One of the group falls into the arms of another, dead.)
>   It ain't just blood and scars.'
(The dead person stands up again and shrugs, others scratch heads.)

>   He told of things folks had never heard,
(Look amazed, eyes wide open.)
>   'Bout life and truth and dreams.
(Punch the air together.)
>   And this guy said that God weren't dead –
(All look up as one, arms folded.)
>   Not even ill, it seems.
(Place hand above eyes and search the skies.)

>   As days rolled by he strolled around
(Turn right and take one step.)
>   With crowds of dames and men.
(Bunch together again as a lively crowd.)
>   And when folks got sick or shot to bits
(All hold arms or shoulders or legs as if injured.)

28

He'd patch 'em up again.

(*Suddenly let go of injured bits and look happy.*)

Even the kids got to like this dude;

(*All suck thumbs.*)

They sat there in the dirt,

(*Sit on floor, or crouch down low, looking up.*)

And folks came round from every town

(*Stand and beckon to audience, inviting them to come and join in.*)

To watch this guy at work.

(*All lean forward and place hand above eyes, watching intently and nodding wisely.*)

But not everyone would listen to

(*Stand back and look angry, fists clenched.*)

The stories this guy spun.

(*Put fingers in ears.*)

The mayor and the guvnor and the sheriff too,

(*One person step forward as each character is mentioned.*)

They didn't like the things he done.

(*These three shake heads while others look at them.*)

They snooped around to hear him out

(*Crouch and spy through imaginary magnifying glasses, held in right hand.*)

But only for detection,

(*They mime scribbling in notebooks.*)

'Cause they figured he was out to rustle their jobs

(*Look around scared.*)

And they sure didn't want no election.

(Hold up hands as if to say 'No way!')

The sheriff hired a posse to track him down

(The sheriff character snaps fingers.)

And bring him up for trial.

(Others turn and form a line.)

But he needn't have bothered, the guy was in town;

(All turn and point ahead.)

A showdown wasn't his style.

(Draw guns and point them at imaginary figure.)

Well, the mayor got scared so he told the crowd

(The mayor character wags his finger at the audience.)

A pack of dirty lies.

(Others look suitably shocked.)

They were easily led and believed what he said

(They nod at one another.)

'Cause they thought he had honest eyes.

(They point at their eyes and flutter their eyelids.)

They arrested the stranger, beat him up good

(They grab imaginary figure and freeze in punching positions, fists raised in the air.)

And threw him into jail.

(They dust off their hands.)

Then the sheriff's men beat him up again,

(Adopt punching positions again, fists raised.)

Just for the hell of it all.

(They turn to the audience and mime sniggering and laughing.)

The sun grew dark over Dead Man's Creek

(All squint and look forward.)

As they whipped him out of town.

(All mime cracking whips.)

They spat on him, but he did not speak,

(All mime spitting at audience.)

So they tied him, gagged and bound.

(Place hands over their own mouths.)

The hangman's noose swung low in the breeze

(They each move their hand in front of their face, as if holding the noose.)

As they hauled him to his feet.

(All reach forward and pull up.)

The trial was brief, the rope cut deep

(They each hold out thumbs and turn them down towards the floor.)

And they left him hangin' in the heat.

(Draw fingers slowly across throat then bow heads.)

The cute little church in the valley below

(Make shape of triangular church roof with arms.)

Stood in the shadow of death.

(Bow heads while still making roof shape.)

As the sun went down they cut him down

(Make chopping movement downwards with right hands.)

His body all bones, no breath.

(Stand with hands open and lean forward as if lowering the body down.)

They carried him away to an unmarked grave,

(*Dig grave.*)

His friends just watched in vain.

(*Sigh and shake heads.*)

The sheriff had said, 'Make sure he's dead'.

(*Sheriff character wag finger at audience.*)

So they lodged a bullet in his brain.

(*Draw guns and point at floor.*)

They washed their hands of the stranger that day.

(*Dust hands off.*)

'That's the last we'll see of him'.

(*Turn backs on audience.*)

And they went away to their poker play,

(*Still facing away mime playing cards in groups.*)

And their whisky, girls and gin.

(*Drink and laugh.*)

Two days went by and things settled down,

(*Turn back and lean on each other in twos.*)

Since the stranger bit the dust.

(*Dust hands off again and nod.*)

There was a poker boom in the Blue Saloon

(*Punch the air excited.*)

And many had gone home bust.

(*Look fed up and downcast.*)

The piana was smooth and business brisk

(*All play piano.*)

The girls still paced the floor.

(*Look bored and swing handbags.*)

The mayor sat back, the sheriff relaxed,

(*Mayor figure puffs on a big cigar, sheriff character hooks fingers under armpits and smiles.*)

When a figure stood poised at the door.

(*All stand suddenly straight, hands on guns at hips.*)

All heads turned at the sudden sound,

(*All look stage right.*)

Each guy reached for his gun.

(*Draw guns.*)

And when that man in white stepped in from the night

(*Look shocked.*)

They figured their judgement had begun.

(*All faint and drop to the floor.*)

But the lean silhouette stood framed in the door.

(*All stand back up and look stage right again.*)

That weren't no ghost, no fraud.

(*Scratch heads in wonder.*)

The stranger smiled like he'd done before,

(*Look shocked and cover eyes.*)

The folks just stared, overawed.

(*Slowly uncover eyes and look stage right, eyes very wide indeed.*)

He showed 'em the scars from the beatin' they gave,

(Hold out arm or leg.)

The rope burn round his neck,

(Pull collars down and show neck.)

The hole where the bullet had lodged in his brain

(Point to side of head.)

To prove that it weren't no trick.

(Shake heads.)

But the best of this tale is yet to come

(Give thumbs up to the audience.)

As he sat and told 'em true,

(Hold out left hand and punch right fist into it.)

That he knew all along he was gonna get hung,

(Hold out hands.)

It was somethin' he just had to do.

(Nod repeatedly.)

It seems this guy just had to die,

(Put hands on heart.)

That's why he came around.

(Look all around for another possibility.)

He weren't no ordinary dude;

(Shake heads and wave hands, palms up.)

God's son had come to town.

(Point upwards and nod.)

Well some of the folks just listened and learned,

(*Lean forward with hand pressed to ear.*)

While others just got plain mad

(*Stand up, stamp foot and look mad.*)

As he told 'em true what they gotta do,

(*Punch fist into palm.*)

To get to know his Dad.

(*Look upwards.*)

He said to trust in what he'd done

(*Show necks again to audience.*)

And in that God above.

(*Look up.*)

Then he plumb got up and just rode out

(*Mime riding along on horses.*)

To tell others about God's love.

(*All punch the air and say out loud, 'Yeah!'*)

A grave situation

Bible reference
Loosely based on Acts 4.1-22

Themes
The first followers of Jesus, the Resurrection and power of Jesus,
also the resurrection of Lazarus, witnessing about who Jesus is

Cast
Posh Judge
Clerk
Peter
John

Props
*None, although you might like to dress the Judge up
in appropriate costume*

*The scene is a court. The Judge sits on a chair or step ladder above everyone else.
His clerk sits on one side and below him. Peter and John have been arrested and
stand stage left at an angle, facing the judge and the audience.*

Judge	Order, order. Silence in court. Now, who have we here?
Clerk	Your honour, these are the defendants – Peter and John – they are accused of preaching about Jesus of Nazareth.
Judge	I see. And what else?
Clerk	Nothing else. That's it.
Judge	Peter and John, is this true?

Peter	Yes.
Judge	And is it a crime?
John	No!
Clerk	They said he had risen from the dead, m'lord.
Judge	Oh I see. Peter and John, is this true?
Peter	Yes it's true. He has risen from the dead.
Judge	No, no. I meant is it true that you said these things?
John	Yes. We did say it and yes it's true.
Judge	I don't wish to know if it's true or not.
John	Why not?
Judge	Why not?
Peter	Yes, why not? Because if it's true, it makes a big difference.
Judge	To what?
John	To everything.
Judge	(*To Clerk*) Does it?
Clerk	Er, I'm not sure, m'lord.
Peter	It does. Because if Jesus is not dead he's alive and if he's alive after you put him to death then that's a miracle. And if that's a miracle then we have to tell people who Jesus is.
Judge	Is that true?
Clerk	Which bit, sir?
Judge	The bit about us putting him to death.
Clerk	Oh yes. Pontius Pilate had him executed.
Judge	And is the other bit true?
Clerk	Which other bit?
Judge	All the other bits, you know, the miracle and Jesus coming back to life and everything.

Peter and John Yes!

Judge Silence in court.

Peter and John (*Sheepishly*) Sorry.

Judge I tell you what I'll do. I'm in a good mood today and I will let you go.

Peter and John Thank you sir.

Judge Providing, you promise to keep this quiet.

Peter To keep what quiet?

Judge Er . . . everything, but especially the bit about Jesus and him being alive.

John Oh but we couldn't do that.

Judge Why not?

John Well, it's amazing news! I mean, d'you know anyone else who came back from the dead?

Judge Er . . . I don't know. Do we?

Clerk Er . . . no, m'lord.

Judge Wait a minute. Yes I do. There was that Lazarus chappie. He'd come back from the dead, hadn't he?

Clerk Shhh!

Judge What d'you mean – 'shhh'?

Clerk I wouldn't bring that up if I were you, m'lord.

Judge Why not?

John Because it was Jesus.

Judge What?

Peter Yes, it was Jesus – he did that – he did a miracle and brought Lazarus back to life when he was dead.

Judge Did he? Ahh, hmmm. He's been busy this Jesus chap, hasn't he?

Peter Yes, he's been healing people, talking to them, helping them. And it's still happening now.

Judge	Is it?
John	Yes. Through us. It's hard to explain but Jesus gave us his power so we can pray for people and help them. So you see we can't keep quiet about it all. We have to pass it on.
Judge	To whom?
Peter	To people. To everyone. The whole world.
Judge	Hmm. This is a grave situation.
Clerk	Is that a joke m'lord?
Judge	What?
Clerk	You said it's a *grave* situation.
Judge	That's not funny.
Clerk	Well, that's what I thought.
Judge	Silence in court! Listen – I've got it. I'll let you go . . .
Peter and John	Thank you again, m'lord.
Judge	If you promise . . .
Peter	Promise what?
Judge	To tell me all about this Jesus of Nazareth.
Clerk	No m'lord, you can't! You've got to stop these men from spreading this around.
Judge	Silence in court! Don't be silly – can't you see that nothing's going to stop these two from talking about Jesus. What I want to do is find out why. Case dismissed.

(They all exit.)

The man who went up

Bible reference

Acts 1.6-11

Themes

Ascension day, Jesus going up to heaven

Cast

Reporter

Man (or Woman)

Props

Microphone and clipboard which the Reporter holds throughout

The Reporter walks on, tidies his hair, clears his throat, looks at the audience as if they are a TV camera and says:

Reporter 3 . . . 2 . . . 1. Ladies and gentlemen, boys and girls, it was on this very spot where it all happened. Just last Thursday, surrounded by a crowd of witnesses – for the first time in history a man, a human being, without the aid of jet power, or rotating blades or a hot-air balloon, without any of that, an ordinary man stood on this very spot and went voooom! (*He looks up*) Right up there!

(*While he has been talking a man/woman has walked on, taken a good look at what's happening and raised a finger in the air as if requesting permission to speak.*)

Man Er, excuse me.

Reporter (*Without even looking at them*) Not now, I'm doing a live broadcast. (*He continues*) Had our cameras been here that day we would have witnessed the impossible. We would have captured on film the human body shooting upwards like a rocket and bursting through the clouds. We would have captured that for the very first time. A world exclusive. Never before seen on film. Worth millions! However, we weren't here, we were filming that stupid dog that was supposed to be able to say sausages – which of course he couldn't, he'd got a cold and lost his voice that day. Huh! Anyway. So now we're left only with a bag full of questions. Who was that man? We don't know. How did he do it?

Man   Er . . .

Reporter   (*Loudly cutting him off and answering his own question*) We don't know. Where did he go?

Man   Er . . .

Reporter   We don't know. And why?

Man   Er, excuse me.

Reporter   Do you mind! This is a live broadcast. An insignificant person, never heard of before, suddenly takes to the skies without the aid of British Airways. Just who was he, we may never know . . .

Man   I do!

Reporter   What?

Man   I do. I know who he was.

Reporter   No you don't!

Man   I do.

Reporter   How?

Man   He was a friend of mine!

Reporter   He wasn't! He didn't have any friends.

Man   He did. He had lots of friends. And he wasn't just an ordinary man, you know. He was an amazing miracle worker, he cured lots of people who were ill, and when people tried to kill him he came back to life again. It's an amazing story. And last Thursday – vooom! He stood on that spot and went back up to heaven, where he'd first come from. His name was Jesus, and he was going back up to God, his father.

41

Reporter   Why don't we know any of this? (*He looks off-stage.*) Who did my research notes? Why haven't we got any of this? We missed a story again! Again! Ohh . . . (*Groans and looks front*) This is news reporter Tom Bewildered, signing off here in Jerusalem where only last week an amazing incident occurred and we didn't know a single thing about it. Drat! Good night.

Man   And he didn't fly up. He didn't flap his arms or anything. He stood on that spot and he said, 'I'll be back'.

Reporter   Shhh!!! Be quiet!

(*Reporter and man both grin at the audience. Both freeze then exit.*)

Bible characters

A tale of two trees

Bible reference
Genesis 1, 2 and 3

Themes
Creation, the garden of Eden, Adam and Eve, the fall, sin

Cast
Narrator
Group of 4–10 children

Props
Chair

A sketch to be performed by a Narrator and a group of children who present the action (described in italics) to the narrative. This piece features the character of Trevor, who also appears later in the book in the sketch 'Trevor the tree'.

Narrator   Once upon a time there was a tiny seed in the ground.
(*All curl up on the floor.*)

It broke through the earth and grew up into a very fine tree.
(*All begin to stand up.*)

Called Trevor.
(*All stick arms up like branches and smile.*)

When it was wet he grew quickly.
(*All flick fingers out fast and say 'Zing!'*)

And when it was dry he grew slowly.
(*Begin to wilt a bit and sigh loudly.*)

Trevor the tree lived in a garden.

(*All make bird and animal sounds.*)

And in the garden there were all kinds of birds

(*All make bird noises and flap arms.*)

And animals.

(*All make animal noises and movements.*)

There were wolves and tigers,

(*Roar and howl.*)

Cats and dogs.

(*Miaow and bark.*)

And for a while – huge dinosaurs,

(*All raise arms like claws.*)

But the dinosaurs didn't last too long – and they all died.

(*All suddenly cough and fall to the floor.*)

Trevor the tree saw and met all these creatures.

(*One child be Trevor, others be birds and animals.*)

Then one day – a man came along.

(*All look shocked.*)

And his name was Adam.

(*All wave and say 'Hello!'*)

He lived in the garden, and it was a good place to be.

(*All put thumbs up and nod.*)

But he soon grew lonely, because he was all on his own.

(*Wipe away tear from eye and sniff.*)

So then Adam the man fell asleep, and Trevor slept too.

(*All place head on hands and sleep.*)

And when they woke up there was a woman.

(*Wake up, look amazed and faint.*)

She had appeared from nowhere and they got a bit of a surprise when they saw her.

(*All get up and rub eyes.*)

The woman was called Eve, and Adam and Trevor and Eve all lived happily together in the garden.

(*All give each other high five.*)

Adam and Eve often climbed up Trevor and pulled

(*One person jump on tree's back.*)

Bits off him, bent his branches and ruffled his leaves.

(*Others pull on arms, etc.*)

Now there was another tree in the garden.

(*All turn their backs on audience.*)

So let's have a look at him for a minute. His name was Angus. Angus Hardbark.

(*Turn to face audience looking angry.*)

And he was a bit gruff.

(*All growl loudly at audience.*)

He was bigger than Trevor,

(*One person jump on a chair.*)

With longer branches and a stronger trunk.

(*That same person stick arms up.*)

And he was full of lots of delicious fruit.

(*Others try and reach up but can't.*)

Adam and Eve loved to look at the fruit,

(*All point and look amazed and impressed.*)

But they weren't allowed to eat it.

(*All look at audience and shake heads.*)

The gardener had told them it was dangerous to eat.

(*All nod solemnly.*)

Very dangerous indeed.

(*Look terrified.*)

It wasn't that the fruit would explode or poison them or give them bright red spots.

(*Some duck, some cover up faces.*)

It was because Angus wasn't their tree, and so the fruit wasn't theirs either. It all belonged to the gardener.

(*All stand up, fold arms and give a big nod.*)

But one day Eve crept up to Angus when he wasn't looking and she stole a piece of his fruit,

(*All tiptoe round in a circle.*)

Took it to Adam and they both had a bite of it.

(*Mime pulling fruit from Angus the tree.*)

Well, Angus Hardbark was very angry about this.

(*Angus the tree looks angry.*)

And all the animals in the garden went quiet,

(*All place fingers to lips and say 'Shhh!'*)

And so did Trevor the tree. And when the gardener found out what had happened

(*All place hands over mouths in shock.*)

He had to send Adam and Eve out of the garden.

(*All point off stage, sending Adam and Eve off.*)

This made the gardener very unhappy, because he wanted to be their best friend, but now he couldn't trust them any more. So Adam and Eve waved goodbye to the garden and to Trevor and they moved away.

(*All wave and exit, or turn away from audience sadly.*)

Shower power

Bible reference
Loosely based on 1 Kings 18.41-46

Themes
Elijah predicts the end of a long drought, God keeps his promises

Cast
Weatherperson
Elijah
Ahab

Props
Fishing equipment, net, rod, box of bait, food hamper, etc.
Wellingtons, thick jumper, overcoat, sun cream, sunglasses, string vest,
sun hat, gloves, swimming goggles, loud colourful socks, two bags of
shopping, bucket of cold water

*The weatherperson may enter and exit as they deliver their lines, or he/she may
remain off-stage and be heard only as a voice-over.*

Weatherperson Good morning, it's five o'clock on a bright and sunny
Saturday and here is the early morning weather fore-
cast – today will remain fine and sunny, with possible
outbreaks of rain in the northern areas.

*(Enter Ahab stage left, loaded down with fishing equipment, a rod, net, box of
bait, hamper. He sets this equipment down, centre stage. Enter Elijah from stage
right.)*

Ahab Mornin' Elijah, comin' fishin'?

Elijah No way, Ahab, not today. Not in this weather.

(*Ahab looks up at the sky.*)

Ahab	What d'you mean? It's perfect weather for fishing, not a cloud in the sky.
Elijah	Sorry Ahab, but the Lord's promised me it's going to rain.
Ahab	Don't be silly, we're in the middle of a drought!
Elijah	Well all I can say is, if you're planning on fishing, take your wellies in case of flooding.
Ahab	Huh, wellies my foot.
Elijah	Well you don't put 'em on your head do you?

(*Elijah goes off-stage. Ahab tuts and sets up a stool and his fishing rod and starts fishing.*)

Weatherperson	Good morning, here is the nine o'clock forecast. The remainder of the morning, through to the afternoon, will remain fine and sunny. The low pressure to the north has moved on. Grab your sunhat, it's gonna be a hot one!

(*Elijah re-enters, wearing his wellingtons. Ahab sees him and laughs.*)

Elijah	How's the fishing, Ahab?
Ahab	Oh not too bad, it's a little too warm for the fish though. Elijah, do you have to wear those?
Elijah	Well I can hardly wade through the water in my trainers, can I?

(*Ahab stops and looks all around.*)

Ahab	Water? What water?

(*Elijah exits, Ahab shakes his head.*)

Weatherperson	Good afternoon. Here is the midday forecast. The weather this afternoon will be extremely hot. Don't leave your pets in the car and if you want to have a barbecue just stick your sausages outside – it's gonna be very very hot!

(Ahab takes off his jumper and puts on his sunglasses. Enter Elijah, pulling on a thick woolly jumper.)

Ahab   Warm enough Elijah?

Elijah   You can laugh now, but I'm sure the weather's on the change.

Ahab   You can say that again, it's gonna get hotter! Haven't you heard the forecast?

(Ahab applies some sun cream.)

Elijah   I've heard what God's told me.

(Elijah exits, Ahab pulls off his shoes and peels off his socks, he smells them and chucks them into the audience.)

Weatherperson *(Now sweating, loosens clothes and huffs and puffs)* Good afternoon. Today is the hottest day of the year. Whew! Temperatures are now up there in the 80s.

(Elijah enters pulling on a heavy coat.)

Ahab   What did I tell you Elijah, face the facts. You might be a great prophet, but everyone gets it wrong sometimes. Come and enjoy the fishing.

Elijah   Haven't got time, sorry. Got to reinforce the roof.

Ahab   Why?

Elijah   Gales, tornados and hurricanes. And hailstones, for when the storm hits.

Ahab   Elijah, d'you want the name of a good doctor?

Elijah   No thanks, but I could do with a good umbrella.

(He exits leaving Ahab tutting and muttering.)

Ahab   Mad . . . Completely ga-ga . . .

Weatherperson Good, whew, afternoon. *(Now wearing a sun hat and fanning himself with news sheets.)* An epidemic of sunstroke is sweeping the nation. One man is seriously ill and many more have been hospitalized. Stay inside and keep cool. Temperatures will – Oh no! – continue to rise.

51

(*Ahab takes off his shirt, underneath he has on a big string vest. Enter Elijah pulling on gloves and swimming goggles.*)

Ahab	Heard the latest news Elijah?
Elijah	Yep.
Ahab	And you still predict rain?
Elijah	Of course. The Lord's told me this drought is gonna stop today. I'd love to chat but I need to stock up with provisions; it's gonna be wet for a long time, you know.
Weatherperson	(*Staggering and with a hanky on his head.*) Good evening. The temperature has just peaked at 90 degrees. Scientists say there'll be no let-up for the foreseeable future. A minute area of low pressure has been spotted over the coast, but it is unlikely to have any effect on the present conditions.

(*Elijah returns carrying two heavy bags of shopping.*)

Elijah	Better head for home Ahab, the storm's likely to break any minute.
Ahab	It's too hot to be indoors, I think I'll sleep under the stars tonight.

(*Elijah exits. Ahab yawns and falls asleep.*)

Weatherperson	(*Off-stage*) Ladies and gentlemen, here is an urgent newsflash. Due to unforeseen circumstances weather conditions have taken a sudden turn for the worse. Storms and gales are sweeping the country and we strongly advise everyone to seek shelter indoors as soon as possible.
Ahab	(*Waking up and looking around*) Wha . . . What? Where? (*Looks off-stage and up*) Oh no!

(*Ahab snatches his fishing rod.*)

Ahab	Elijah was right! I'd better get back. How did he know it was gonna change? (*He heads off-stage*) I'd better get back before it starts to . . . (*He is splashed with water from off-stage*) . . . rain!

Weatherperson So, here is the final forecast – God's word can be trusted, even when people around you tell you otherwise. You can rely on him, he'll never let you down. Good night.

(*Weatherperson exits.*)

The Planimals meet Shad, Shack and Bed

Bible reference
Daniel 3.1-30

Themes
The story of Shadrach, Meshach and Abednego, faith and courage, worshipping God

Cast
Narrator
Dog Rose
Pussy Willow
Goose Grass
Dandy Lion
Tiger Lily
Monkey Puzzle
Horse Chestnut

Props
None

The cast respond to the Narrator with the actions and noises described in italics. Begin with them all standing on stage in a line. There can be as many as you want presenting the piece, and they may all do the different characters together if you prefer.

Narrator   Welcome to Planimaland. The place where the Planimals live. There's Dog Rose . . .

(*Dog Rose stands up and barks and pants.*)

> And Pussy Willow . . .

(*Pussy Willow stands up and miaows and washes her face.*)

> And Goose Grass

(*Goose Grass stands up and says: 'Honk, honk!'*)

> And Spider Plant

(*Every one runs their fingers over each other.*)

> And Dandy Lion

(*Dandy Lion stands up and roars in a rather posh and lazy way.*)

> And Tiger Lily

(*Tiger Lily roars more ferociously and everyone jumps.*)

> And big Horse Chestnut tree

(*Horse Chestnut shakes head and makes a 'Brrrrr' noise by flapping lips like a horse.*)

> And of course, Monkey Puzzle.

(*Monkey Puzzle stands up and says: 'Ooh ooh, ahh ahh!' and scratches armpits.*)

> Now one day, Dandy Lion

(*Dandy Lion stands up and roars in a rather posh and lazy way.*)

> Was feeling a bit scared.

(*All bite nails.*)

> Because he had to go to the dentist.

(*All slap hand over mouth.*)

> And Monkey Puzzle

(*Monkey Puzzle stands up and says: 'Ooh ooh, ahh ahh!' and scratches armpits.*)

> Was feeling a bit scared too.

(*All bite nails.*)

> Because he had to go to the optician.

(*All slap hands over eyes.*)

And they were very nervous about it.

(*All shake on the spot.*)

'Don't panic,' said the big Horse Chestnut tree,

(*Horse Chestnut shakes head and makes a 'Brrrrr' noise by flapping lips like a horse.*)

'Come under my branches and we'll have a nice cup of tea'.

(*All make a slurping noise and mime drinking tea.*)

'And I'll tell you a story to cheer you up'.

(*All put on big smiles.*)

So all the Planimals

(*All the Planimals make their noises together.*)

Came and sat in the shade of Horse Chestnut

(*Horse Chestnut shakes head and makes a 'Brrrrr' noise by flapping lips like a horse.*)

And he told them the story of Shadrach, Meshach and Abednego. Or Shad, Shack and Bed for short.

(*Everyone says 'Shad, Shack and Bed!'*)

They were good friends with each other and good friends with God too,

(*Everyone squashes together looking friendly and they put their thumbs up.*)

Just like the Planimals.

(*All the Planimals make their noises together.*)

But one day their king said to them, 'You can't worship God any more, or pray to him, or sing songs about him, you've got to worship me instead!'

(*All look shocked and say 'Ha!'*)

So, Shad, Shack and Bed were very scared.

(*Bite nails.*)

But they couldn't stop praying to God, because he was their friend, so the king said, 'Right! Guards, throw them into the big fiery furnace!' So they threw Shad, Shack and Bed into the fire and the flames – and it was very, very hot!

(*All fan themselves, huff and puff and wipe sweat from brows.*)

But, God was looking down on it all

(*All lean forward and look down, hand held above eyes.*)

And he looked after Shad, Shack and Bed, and even though they should have been burned up – the fire didn't hurt them at all.

(*Everyone applaud loudly and cheer.*)

And when the king opened the door of the furnace they walked out – perfectly okay! They didn't even smell of smoke!

(*Everyone sniffs loudly.*)

'Well', said the king, 'your God is amazing. He's looking after you. From now I think everyone should worship him'. And so that's what happened.

(*All shout 'AMEN!'*)

When he'd finished his story Horse Chestnut

(*Horse Chestnut shakes head and makes a 'Brrrrr' noise by flapping lips like a horse.*)

Looked at Monkey Puzzle

(*Monkey Puzzle stands up and says: 'Ooh ooh, ahh ahh!' and scratches armpits.*)

And Dandy Lion.

(*Dandy Lion stands up and roars in a rather posh and lazy way.*)

They still looked a little scared.

(*Bite nails.*)

'Don't worry', he said, 'I'm sure that God wants to help you too'. And all the Planimals agreed.

(*All the Planimals make their noises together.*)

The Planimals meet Dan and the lions

Bible reference
Daniel 6

Themes
The story of Daniel in the lions' den, being brave,
having faith and courage, praying

Cast
Narrator
Dog Rose
Pussy Willow
Goose Grass
Dandy Lion
Tiger Lily
Monkey Puzzle
Horse Chestnut

Props
None

*The cast respond to the Narrator with the actions and noises described in italics.
Begin with them all standing on stage in a line. There can be as many as you
want presenting the piece, and they may all do the different characters together if
you prefer.*

Narrator Welcome to Planimaland. The place where the Planimals
live. There's Dog Rose . . .

(Dog Rose stands up and barks and pants.)

And Pussy Willow . . .

(Pussy Willow stands up and miaows and washes her face.)

And Goose Grass

(Goose Grass stands up and says: 'Honk, honk!')

And Spider Plant

(Every one runs their fingers over each other.)

And Dandy Lion

(Dandy Lion stands up and roars in a rather posh and lazy way.)

And Tiger Lily

(Tiger Lily roars more ferociously and everyone jumps.)

And big Horse Chestnut tree,

(Horse Chestnut shakes head and makes a 'Brrrrr' noise by flapping lips like a horse.)

And of course, Monkey Puzzle.

(Monkey Puzzle stands up and says: 'Ooh ooh, ahh ahh!' and scratches armpits.)

Now one day, in the summer when it was very hot, all the Planimals

(All the Planimals make their noises together.)

Gathered for shade under Horse Chestnut.

(Horse Chestnut shakes head and makes a 'Brrrrr' noise by flapping lips like a horse.)

'There are some very famous lions in the Bible', said Horse Chestnut.

(Horse Chestnut shakes head and makes a 'Brrrrr' noise by flapping lips like a horse.)

Dandy Lion looked very pleased with himself.

(Dandy Lion stands up and roars in a rather posh and lazy way.)

'Tell us about it', said all the Planimals.

(*All the Planimals make their noises together.*)

So Horse Chestnut

(*Horse Chestnut shakes head and makes a 'Brrrrr' noise by flapping lips like a horse.*)

Opened up his big blue Bible and began to read,

(*They all mime opening a very big book.*)

'Once there was a brave man called Daniel'.

(*They all cheer.*)

He worked for a king, in a land far, far away.

(*All look off into the distance.*)

Daniel worked in the royal court

(*All bow.*)

And he prayed to God

(*All kneel, place hands together and bow heads then stand again.*)

Twice a day;

(*They all kneel, pray, stand up and then kneel again and pray.*)

No, more than that, three times a day.

(*They all sigh then kneel and pray and stand three times very quickly.*)

He was a good man

(*They all punch the air and say 'Yes!'*)

But some of the other men in the king's courts were not good men.

(*All hiss loudly, and pull a mean face.*)

They told lies about people

(*Whisper to each other in twos.*)

And they were not happy that brave Daniel

(*All cheer.*)

Prayed

(*All kneel, place hands together and bow heads then stand again.*)

Three times every day.

(*They all sigh then kneel and pray and stand three times very quickly.*)

So they went to the king, bowed low,

(*All bow.*)

And said, 'Daniel doesn't worship you, he worships his God instead!'

(*All wag finger as if gossiping.*)

Well, the king was horrified

(*All look horrified.*)

And he threw Daniel into the lions' den!

(*All point off stage and roar loudly.*)

But the bad guys

(*All hiss.*)

Didn't know that the lions

(*All roar loudly.*)

Were on Daniel's side.

(*All cheer.*)

And when they saw Daniel the lions did an amazing thing. They went to sleep!

(*All lean on each other and snore loudly.*)

They didn't eat brave Daniel.

(*All cheer.*)

Instead they did what God told them to: they lay down, very quietly, and they went to sleep.

(*All snore again.*)

'Lions don't snore, they roar!'

(*All roar angrily and loudly.*)

Said Dandy Lion.

(*Dandy Lion stands up and roars in a rather posh and lazy way.*)

> Ah, but these were very special lions. They only ate bad guys. So when the King threw the bad guys into the lions' den, the lions scoffed the lot!

(*All chomp very loudly.*)

> And Daniel came out alive, and lived happily ever after.

(*All cheer.*)

> Then, Horse Chestnut

(*Horse Chestnut shakes head and makes a 'Brrrrr' noise by flapping lips like a horse.*)

> Closed his big blue Bible and all the Planimals

(*All the Planimals make their noises together.*)

> Curled up in the shade of his big branches and dozed off to sleep themselves.

(*All curl up and snore.*)

Eyes open

Bible reference
John 9.1-11

Themes
Healing, faith, the power of Jesus to change lives,
the healing of a blind man

Cast
Jesus
Blind person
Two disciples, Mary and Peter
A crowd of eight or more

Props
None

This is a large-group mime, for twelve or more people. There are sections where your group should be encouraged to choose the action for themselves, e.g. what character they want to play and how they might react at different points in the story; they can decide some of these things. This piece need not necessarily be performed to an audience; it can just be experiential, or used as a class or workshop exercise, or to help experience the Bible story afresh. This style could be adopted for other similar Bible stories.

Action

The scene is a town: lots of people sitting around, playing games, buying and selling at street stalls.

Get everyone to decide what sort of person they would like to be. Perhaps a Roman soldier on guard, or a street salesperson, or a shopper, or someone sitting or sleeping or playing cards in a group. Or just sitting or standing around chatting or gossiping.

Appoint one person to be a blind person, male or female, and another to be Jesus and two more to be followers of Jesus: one male, Peter, one female, Mary.

Start playing some gentle background music and ask everyone to begin miming this scene. If they want to pretend they are talking with someone, tell them to move their lips and talk rubbish silently so it will look as if they are talking, but there will be no sound.

Let the scene run for a little bit then get the blind person to walk on, eyes open and glazed and fixed, one hand out to the front as if feeling their way forward. Tell them to try not to move their eyes or look as if they can see the other people; if they bump into anyone, that's okay, they should just wave an apologetic hand. Tell them to move to an empty spot and sit down. Everyone else should carry on as normal, not really paying much attention to the blind person.

Now ask Jesus, Mary and Peter to walk on together. They should stop in the middle of everyone and Jesus then drops down and begins writing in the dirt, as he explains something to Mary and Peter. Again, this should be silent and Jesus should just move his lips as if talking. Slowly others begin to notice Jesus and overhear what he is saying. Then they cautiously and slowly begin to move closer and gather round. As they do this the blind person also overhears, but instead of looking the blind person cocks an ear in the direction of Jesus and the others. Slowly the blind person stands up and, with hands held out front to feel the way he or she (if 'he'/'his'/'him' will be used hereafter as shorthand for 's/he',, etc.) walks towards the sound. On the way the blind person trips over someone who is crouching down near Jesus and nearly falls over. Some of the others grab the blind person and steady him and he smiles apologetically. Then Jesus sees the blind person, stands up and comes over. He takes the blind person's hands and places them on his face so the blind person can feel what Jesus looks like. Jesus then spits on his hands while the blind person waits quietly and then he places one handful of spit on one of the blind person's eyes. The blind person grimaces, recoils and tries to run off, but Mary and Peter grab him and reassure him and hold him there. Jesus places both hands over the blind person's eyes and rubs them gently. Then he leads the blind person, who now has his eyes shut, towards an imaginary trough of water. Everyone else watches, silent and wide-eyed. Jesus stops the blind person at the trough and Jesus himself reaches in, scoops up some water and tastes it in his hand. Then he takes the blind person's hand, stretches it out and touches the water with it. The blind person begins to scoop up handfuls of water and wash the spit out of his eyes; again and again the blind person scoops up water and washes his face, all the time keeping his eyes tightly shut. Eventually he stops, looks front and opens his eyes. Then it gradually dawns on him – he can see! He suddenly opens his eyes very wide, freezes for a moment looking amazed, then he slams his hands over his eyes in reaction to the sudden bright daylight. Then he uncovers his eyes again, looks round, then slams his hands over again. Then he looks round, again and begins spinning around on the spot. He starts to smile and laugh, then he sees other people and runs around to them, looking right in their faces and at their clothes and shoes. He runs around madly and the people look amazed, they mime talking hurriedly to each other as they realize what has happened.

Eventually the blind person ends up standing suddenly in front of Jesus. He stops, reaches out, touches Jesus' face and begins to realize that this is the man who has given him back his sight. He suddenly drops to his knees, almost in tears and he grabs onto Jesus' legs very tightly, never wanting to let go, his head bowed in humble thanks. Jesus tries gently to prise him off his legs, but the blind person holds on tightly and eventually Jesus tumbles backwards and over onto the ground. The people rush in and help both Jesus and the blind person to stand up again. The blind person steps back from the crowd, looks around at everything, then opens his arms wide at everyone, and after a moment's pause the people all rush in and swamp him in one huge hug! Freeze as the man disappears inside the pile of bodies.

End.

Trevor the tree

Bible reference
Luke 19.1-10

Themes
The story of Jesus meeting Zacchaeus, friendship with Jesus,
Jesus cares for everyone

Cast
Narrator
Trevor the tree
Zac

Props
None

This a lively retelling of the story of Zacchaeus. There is no need for anyone to portray Jesus, this is done through Zac's reaction and mime. You might like to play some cartoon-style music in the background behind the narrative to jolly the piece along.

Narrator   Meet Trevor,

(*Trevor walks on and waves.*)

Trevor the tree.

(*He suddenly adopts a tree pose.*)

Lots of people liked Trevor the tree. Children,

(*Zac runs on acting like a small child. He sees Trevor and swings on his arm as if it is a branch.*)

Teenagers,

(*Zac becomes a teenager, looks cool, sucks on a fag and stubs it out on Trevor. Trevor winces and slaps Zac.*)

Dogs,

(*Zac becomes a dog and barks and pants and wees against Trevor's leg. Trevor lifts his leg and shakes it.*)

And one day a little man climbed up Trevor the tree.

(*Zac jumps on Trevor's back. Trevor looks in pain.*)

But this chap didn't normally go climbing trees.

(*Zac jumps down and Trevor looks relieved and wipes his brow.*)

His name was Zac and he normally worked in an office.

(*Zac mimes office work. Trevor peeps over his shoulder and watches as he works.*)

But on this day he did climb the tree.

(*Zac jumps back and leaps on Trevor's back, Trevor only just manages to become a tree again just in time.*)

And the reason he did this was so that he could see someone.

(*Zac points excitedly and puts his hands over Trevor's face and eyes as he steadies himself.*)

A man called Jesus had come to town and everyone wanted to see him.

(*Trevor pushes Zac's hand away so that he can have a good look too. Zac waves.*)

Suddenly, Jesus looked up at the tree.

(*Zac and Trevor both look shocked and their mouths drop open in horror.*)

Jesus asked Zac if he could have a cup of tea.

(*Zac is so shocked he falls off Trevor. Then they both search in their pockets and look up and shake their heads.*)

But Zac didn't have any tea with him, so he grabbed Jesus by the arm and pulled him all the way home to his house.

(*Zac mimes pulling Jesus and running on the spot while Trevor becomes the house, or the door of the house. They open the door and walk in.*)

And as they sat at Zac's table drinking tea and eating beans on toast,

(*Trevor becomes the table and Zac drinks tea and talks to Jesus. Trevor watches them both.*)

Zac and Jesus became the best of friends.

(*They mime shaking hands. Trevor looks at the audience and nods and grins happily.*)

And that's the story of Zac.

(*They all stand and bow.*)

Jairus' daughter

Bible reference
Luke 8.40-56

Themes
Two stories of Jesus healing people, Jesus' compassion and power,
Jesus has time for everyone

Cast
One or two narrators

Four or more actors

Props
None

*A sketch for one or two narrators and a group who respond to the lines of
narrative. This is in fact two sketches rolled into one! The story of Jairus'
daughter and the story of the woman who touched the hem of Jesus' robe. It can
be performed as one long piece, or broken up into the two separate stories by
removing the middle section about the woman who touched the hem.*

Narrator   Once there was a little girl who loved to play games.

(All run on stage and play games noisily.)

She had lots of friends.

(All hug, give each other five, etc.)

But one day she started to feel quite ill.

(All hold stomach and say 'Ow!')

First, her arm started to hurt.

(Quickly change and hold arm, and say 'Ow!')

Then her leg.

(*Then hold leg and say 'Ow!'*)

Then her tummy.

(*Then hold tummy and say 'Ow!'*)

Then all over.

(*Hold all different bits and say 'Ow! Ow! Ow!'*)

Now, her dad was a very important man.

(*All stand to attention and bow.*)

His name was Jairus and he was very wise,

(*All stroke chins deep in thought, saying 'Hmmmmm'.*)

Very upright,

(*All stand up as tall and straight as possible.*)

And very religious.

(*All put hands together in prayer position and say, 'A-a-amen'.*)

He also had lots of friends.

(*All shake hands looking dignified, two of the group give each other five then realize and become dignified like the others and shake hands.*)

And when he saw how ill his daughter was

(*Look very worried.*)

He ran to find one of them.

(*Freeze in running positions.*)

When he found his friend, Jairus fell down on the floor

(*All drop down.*)

And begged for his help.

(*All look up and plead with hands clasped.*)

'Please come and help my daughter', he said. 'She's not well'.

(*All say 'Pleeeeeeeeeeease?'*)

Jairus' friend was called Jesus and he promised to come and help.

(*All look happy, jump up and punch the air and say 'Yes!'.*)

Meanwhile Jairus' daughter got worse

(*Hold stomachs and groan.*)

And worse

(*Groan louder.*)

And worse.

(*Groan louder again.*)

As Jesus walked along lots of his friends stopped him to say hello.

(*Wave and all say together, 'Hello!'*)

And before long there were so many people it was all a bit of a squash.

(*All squash together and suck in cheeks.*)

All of a sudden Jesus stopped.

(*All say 'Huh!' as if catching their breath and freeze in mid-walking pose, like statues.*)

And then Jesus said, 'Who touched me?'

(*All put their hands up and say 'Me!'*)

They all said this because they were all jammed together so tightly

(*Squash together really, really tightly.*)

That everyone was touching everyone else.

(*All intertwine bodies with each other.*)

'No', he said. 'I mean someone reached out for my help'.

(*All shake heads, hold up hands and say 'Not me'.*)

They looked all around.

(*All look around, hand above eyes.*)

They looked high,

(*All look up high.*)

They looked low.

(*All look at the floor.*)

They looked left,

(*All look right except one person on the right end of the line, who says 'Ahem!' and points them in the opposite direction. They then all look sheepish and look left.*)

They looked right.

(*All look right.*)

Then a woman stepped forward

(*One of the group, a female, steps forward. Others look shocked.*)

And said,

(*That person says 'It was me'.*)

She had been very ill for a long time and she had stretched out her hand and touched Jesus.

(*The person stretches out her right hand and arm out towards the audience. The rest of the group do this in their line behind her. They all strain as they reach out.*)

'How do you feel now?' Jesus asked.

(*One person steps forward and takes the woman's pulse. Another one or two come forward and mime examining her through a magnifying glass. The woman thinks for a second, then nods and says 'Much better!'*)

And indeed she was.

(*All leap in the air happily.*)

Just then a man pushed his way through the crowd.

(*One of the group runs out the front and gasps: 'Jairus' daughter is dead'. All the group gasp and repeat together, 'Jairus' daughter is dead'.*)

But Jesus said, 'Don't worry. She's only asleep!'

(*All sleep on each other, head on next person's shoulder.*)

At Jairus' house everyone was very upset.

(*All weep and cry.*)

But Jesus went into the room and shut the door.

(*All mime shutting door and then say 'Bang!'*)

Outside the people wondered what was happening.

(*All scratch heads and look perplexed.*)

They paced up and down,

(*All pace up and down.*)

They listened at the door.

(*All listen at the door.*)

They drank cups of tea,

(*All drink tea with a slurping noise.*)

They even watched 'Neighbours'.

(*All doze off to sleep.*)

Then all of a sudden the door opened and there was Jairus' daughter;

(*All look amazed.*)

She was alive again!

(*Leap in the air and freeze looking very happy.*)

This is your life

Bible reference

Luke 5.27-32

Themes

Jesus calls Matthew to follow him, Jesus can change our lives,
God's forgiveness for the things we do wrong

Cast

TV host
Matthew
Jake
Martha
Two off-stage voice-overs

Props

Shopping bag, big red book, money, metal plate, chair, large plastic toy
knife, big dusty black book, sound effects for a cork being pulled out of
a bottle and liquid being poured

*A street somewhere. Matthew stands looking around, shopping bag in hand. TV
host sidles up from behind, big red book in hand, looking suspicious. When he gets
right behind Matthew he pounces.*

Host	Matthew? Matthew Levi?
Matthew	(*Startled*) Yes?
Host	Matthew Levi, you thought you'd come out shopping this morning to buy your weekly supply of peanut butter and beetroot sandwiches, but no, Matthew Levi, Tax Collector extraordinaire, today – this is your life!

(*Matthew is taken aback and he tries to run away but the host grabs him and ushers him to a nearby chair.*)

Host	Yes Matthew, today this *is* your life. And for you that means going back 27 years to a remote fishing village where you were born the only child of Bartholomew and Sarah – a delightful, humble couple who struggled and scraped to give you the best education and upbringing they could. However, they can't be with us tonight Matthew, unfortunately you had them both imprisoned when they could no longer afford to pay their taxes. But they send their best wishes.

(*Matthew shuffles awkwardly in his seat.*)

Matthew	Well that is true of course but . . .
Host	The years passed by and soon you left your simple past behind you, and leaving home you began working for the Romans.
Matthew	They were good employers.
Host	Yes, and the cruel, vicious oppressors of your own people.
Matthew	I only worked part-time at first . . .
Host	But not for long. And I wonder Matthew, can you identify this familiar sound?

(*There is the sound of coins falling onto a metal dish. Matthew nods gloomily.*)

Host	Yes, the sum of your life's work – money. You eagerly embarked on a selfish, greedy trail of collecting taxes from your fellow Jews, overcharging and short-changing.
Matthew	Not every customer.
Host	No, some of them slipped through, but you fleeced most of them. Which is where our next memorable object comes in. Matthew, do you recognize this familiar piece?

(Host pulls out a huge carving knife. Matthew looks shocked and tries to shush the host as he goes on.)

Host Yes, of course, it's the weapon you used to deal with awkward customers – those who couldn't afford to pay your extravagant taxes. From then on you went from strength to strength, no deal was too dirty for you, no customers too poor to be ripped off. And today, especially for this occasion, from Jewish archives we have traced this unique specimen.

(Host opens a large dusty black book. Matthew tries to hide his embarrassed face.)

Host Yes Matt, I'm sure the happy memories are flooding back – it's your original accounts book. May I read a random extract?

Matthew No!

Host Thank you. August 25th. Taxes acquired that day, £500 – a good morning's work. Money handed over to your Roman employers – £50. *(He is puzzled.)* Which leaves an outstanding balance of £450 unaccounted for . . .

Matthew *(Clears his throat heavily.)* Oh, er . . . er . . . expenses. Yes, expenses.

Host Oh! Yes. I see. Of course in your new life you soon made plenty of important new friends and this sound soon became a prominent part of your life.

(There is the sound of bottles clinking and a cork being removed and wine poured.)

Host Yes, feast after feast, and party after party followed in quick succession and all paid for by the poor taxpayers you were robbing. And today, Matthew, we've flown out two of your old customers especially for this occasion. They were very keen to see you again.

(Enter two irate customers, they come in behind the host.)

Jake Where is he? I'll kill him.

Martha Not until I break his legs and pull off his earlobes.

Jake	There he is! You diddled me out of 5,000 quid, where is it?
Martha	And all those times you overcharged me, I had to sell my grandad in order to pay you!
Jake	Yeah, and what about my coat, and you even had the shirt off my back one time!
Host	Yes, yes, thank you very much Jake and Martha Angry!

(*He holds them back and ushers them off while Matthew cowers behind his chair.*)

Host	I bet that was a nice surprise, I guess you didn't expect to see them again?

(*Matthew nervously sits back down again.*)

Host	We met up with a few more of your closest friends . . .

(*Matthew leaps up again and runs behind the chair.*)

Host	No, no, they couldn't be with us today but they sent this message.
Voice-over 1	Matthew? Matthew Levi? Yes. I remember him. Aggghhhhhhhh! No! Aggghhhhh! Let me out of here!
Host	Happy times, eh, Matthew? And just at a time when things seemed to be going really well – at a time when you had no friends – no family – your life was a succession of heavy drinking and beating up people – and you were even wanted by the Romans for cheating them – just as you seemed to have reached your pinnacle . . . a dramatic moment transformed your life. Remember this voice?
Voice-over 2	Matthew, follow me.

(*Matthew looks suddenly relieved and he smiles for the first time.*)

Host	Yes, at a point when you had reached your lowest, when no one else wanted to know you, that man walked into your life, and you've never been the same since. Do you remember that day?

(*Matthew nods.*)

Matthew   I was sitting there in my office and he just walked right in, no knocking or nothing. We had a chat and the next thing you know I'd invited him round for a party. He said he'd only come if I invited every other tax collector in the neighbourhood along as well. So I did! Then he told me to follow him, and that was the last time I saw my tax office. He didn't seem at all bothered about what I'd been up to, so I had to go with him just to see what he was all about.

Host   Matthew Levi, tax collector, liar, thief, cheat, fiddler, conman, corrupter of the poor – but now forgiven. (*He holds out his red book for Matthew to take.*) This is your life.

(*All freeze or exit, Matthew thumbing through the book.*)

The woman with the bad back

Bible reference

Luke 13.10-17

Themes

Jesus has power to heal and change lives,
Jesus heals a woman on the Sabbath.

Cast

Two puppets

1

2, the woman who has been healed of a bad back

Props

Two puppets and the appropriate set for presenting the piece

This sketch was first presented using hand puppets with actors supplying the voices. It may of course be acted live but, if doing so, do add your own stage directions to make the dialogue a little more animated. The scene is a dialogue in the street.

1	Excuse me! Excuse me! Aren't you the woman with the bad back?
2	Me?
1	Yes.
2	No.
1	Oh! Are you sure?
2	Yes.

1   Oh, okay then, bye.

(*1 walks off.*)

2   I used to be.

(*1 zooms back on.*)

1   What?

2   I used to be the woman with the bad back.

1   You mean you got better?

2   No.

1   No?

2   No. Jesus fixed me.

1   He fixed you?

2   Yes, I used to be bent over like this. (*She bends over.*) And I couldn't walk straight, I'd been like that for a long time.

1   How long? A week?

2   Nope.

1   A month?

2   Nope.

1   Not a whole year?

2   Nope – 18 years!

1   Wow! (*1 falls over stunned, then quickly gets up again.*) That's a long time.

2   Then I saw Jesus in the synagogue and he touched me and I went from here . . .

(*She bends over.*)

2   To here! (*She straightens up.*) Instantly!

1   Wowwwww! (*Falls over again.*) Do that again!

2   I went from here (*She bends over.*) To here! (*She straightens up.*)

1   I bet everyone was amazed.

2   They were annoyed.

1   Were they?

2   Some of them were, yes. They told Jesus off, they said that it wasn't fair of him to make me better on the Sabbath day when we're all supposed to be having a day off.

1   What did Jesus say?

2   He said that was silly. He likes making people better. And it's silly not to help people every day of the week. And the people who were telling him off looked after their cows on a Sabbath, so it was no use pretending that they didn't. That's what God wants, he doesn't want a lot of rules and regulations, he wants people to love him and to care for other people.

1   Wowww! Jesus is clever isn't he? He knows a lot of things. By the way, how's your back now?

2   Brilliant! Look – I can even do this. (*She does some acrobatic movement as they go off.*)

Talking sense

Bible reference
Acts 2

Themes
The day of Pentecost, the Holy Spirit, Peter and the disciples preach to the crowds and the Church is born

Cast
1, 2 and 3 (ordinary people)

Props
None

This sketch could be performed by live actors or by glove puppets. 1 and 2 walk on talking, they are on a road near Jerusalem.

1   Hey! Have you heard what's going on in town?

2   No.

1   Mad panic. You know there's all those foreigners around, because of the festival?

2   Yes, but they come every year – it's always chaos.

1   Not like this it isn't. Remember Peter?

2   Oh, you mean the fisherman whose name changed?

1   That's the one. Well he's preaching.

2   What! Don't be silly. He's not a preacher.

1   He is now.

2   What's he preaching about?

1	Jesus of Nazareth.
2	No! Don't be silly.
1	Yep.
2	I bet there aren't many people listening.
1	Only about 10,000.
2	What! Don't be silly.
1	Look will you stop telling me not to be silly? I'm not being silly.
2	Are you sure?
1	Yes! I'm sure I'm not being silly; and I'm sure that Peter, who used to be Simon, who used to be a fisherman, who used to be scared, who used to be shy, is now a preacher shouting his head off in front of thousands of people – who are all listening.
2	Well, I bet it doesn't make any difference. I bet no one gets converted.
1	3,000.
2	3,000 what?
1	3,000 people – that's how many he's converted.
2	Don't be silly! He couldn't convert my gas cooker to electric.
1	I am not being silly!!
2	Hang on a minute – you said the town was full of foreigners.
1	That's right.
2	And you said they were all listening.
1	That's right.
2	Don't be silly!
1	I'm going to flick your ear if you say that again.
2	Well, how can they all hear, and how can they all understand? They come from different countries don't they?
1	Ah well, that's where the others come in.
2	Which others?

1   Peter's friends – James, John, Andrew, Philip – all Jesus' disciples.

2   You mean that rough and ready bunch of men who can't do anything except argue with each other.

1   That's them. Well, now they're interpreting everything Peter says.

2   They're what?

1   Everything Peter says is being translated into different languages by the disciples so that everybody in the town can hear what Peter is saying.

2   You're mad.

1   Well at least you've stopped calling me silly.

2   And you're silly. Ow! (*1 flicks his ear.*)

1   I warned you.

2   Look, let me get this straight. There's a group of men in the town, who used to be scared stiff, who could hardly speak their own language never mind anyone else's, and now they're talking to thousands of people.

1   That's about it. Wait a minute! Where are you going?

2   If this is true – it's amazing. It's unbelievable. And whatever those guys are on, I want some of it, 'cause things like this don't just happen. This I have got to see.

(*He exits.*)

1   Great! Now what am I gonna do? Oh hello.

(*Enter 3.*)

1   Hey! Have you heard what's going on in the town?

3   No.

1   Remember Peter?

3   Oh, you mean the fisherman whose name changed?

1   That's the one. Well he's preaching.

3   What! Don't be silly.

1   I am not being silly . . . Look. You won't believe me but there's something amazing going on in Jerusalem – Peter and his friends are telling thousands of people about Jesus.

3   I don't believe you!

1   What did I tell you? Come on.

3   Where are we going?

1   Well, I'm fed up of talking about it, and having people tell me I'm silly. It's time we saw for ourselves. Let's go and hear Peter doing what he could never do.

3   What's that?

1   Talk some sense to an awful lot of people.

3   Now that must be a miracle!

(*They exit.*)

Parables

Frisk and Dexter
and the injured man

Bible reference
Luke 10.25-37

Themes
The parable of the good Samaritan,
helping one another, caring for people in need

Cast
Narrator

Frisk

Dexter

Snooty Priest

The good Samaritan, who helps the imaginary injured man

Props
Long black coat, sunglasses, notebook and pencil, bell to make the
sound of the phone (optional)

This is a retelling of the Good Samaritan parable. The two detectives, particularly Dexter, should be cool. Begin with the Narrator standing alone on stage, stage left.

Narrator   Frisk and Dexter ran a time-travel investigation agency. They were detectives who could investigate any crime from any time. When the purple phone on Dexter's desk rang like an old school bell, they knew that a case from history was calling them. Dexter wore a long black coat and had a dog called Bilko.

(*Dexter walks on wearing a long black coat. He mimes pulling a dog on a lead.*)

Frisk wore small, dark glasses and always carried a notebook.

(*Frisk walks on putting on his dark glasses.*)

One day the purple phone rang . . .

(*Dexter mimes picking up a phone.*)

And Frisk and Dexter found themselves standing on a dry dusty road in a dry dusty valley.

(*They cough silently and wave the dust from their faces and eyes.*)

The wind whistled around,

(*Narrator and Frisk and Dexter make the sound of wind whistling around. Frisk and Dexter battle against the wind and shield their eyes from the hot sun, high in the sky.*)

And they started to fry in the hot desert sun.

(*Frisk mimes taking out an egg and he breaks it on a rock and makes the sound of it frying.*)

Suddenly they heard a voice groan. 'Ughhh!'

Frisk   Hey look!

Narrator Said Frisk pointing beside the road.

(*Frisk indeed does point.*)

They ran over to the side, where they found a man lying under a pile of rocks.

(*They run on the spot and then screech to a halt, leaning back as they stop.*)

The man had been beaten up and robbed.

Frisk   Let's help him up

Narrator Said Frisk.

(*They mime lifting big rocks off the man.*)

Dexter suddenly stopped and listened.

(*Dexter freezes, holding the rock.*)

Dexter   Listen, someone's coming. Hide!

(*Dexter throws his rock over his shoulder and it hits the Narrator.*)

Narrator   Ow!

(*Narrator falls over and Frisk and Dexter hide behind him. Narrator gets up, rubbing his head.*)

While they watched a very religious priest went past, but he didn't stop to help the man.

(*Frisk and Dexter come out of hiding and walk centre stage.*)

Frisk   He went straight past and didn't help the injured man.

Narrator   Said Frisk.

Dexter   Some people are like that.

Narrator   Said Dexter. Just then they heard the sound of falling rocks. They panicked.

(*Frisk dives behind the Narrator again.*)

Dexter   I'm not going to panic. (*Looking off-stage*) They could be the bad guys who attacked this man. I'm going after them.

Narrator   And he ran off. Just then another man appeared. As Frisk watched . . .

(*Frisk's head pops out from behind the Narrator.*)

He helped the man who'd been attacked and took him off to safety.

(*Frisk watches this, then Dexter comes racing back on.*)

Frisk   Did you find the bad guys?

Narrator   Said Frisk, but Dexter shook his head.

Dexter   They got away, but I found this note in the dust.

Narrator   What's it say?

Frisk   Said the Narrator.

(*The Narrator and Dexter look at Frisk, a little confused by this. Then Dexter hands the Narrator the note.*)

Narrator   Oh. It says, 'Which of you was a good friend to Dougal?'

Frisk   Who's Dougal?

Narrator   The injured man. 'Which of you acted like a good friend to him?'

(They scratch their heads and think for a second then Frisk points at Dexter and Dexter points at Frisk.)

    Nope. It says, 'Marmaduke'.

Frisk   Who's Marmaduke?

Narrator   That man who helped him to safety.

Frisk   Oh, does it say anything else? Like Frisk and Dexter acted like quite good friends?

Narrator   Nope. It says, 'Remember the story and do the same yourself next time'.

Dexter   Oh. Anything else?

Narrator   Yes. It says: The end – get off quick.

(They all turn to face the audience and bow and run off.)

Frisk and Dexter and the throttled man

Bible reference
Matthew 18.21-35

Themes
Forgiving one another, not holding a grudge or nursing anger

Cast
Narrator

Frisk

Dexter

Derek

Pete

Two extras for the line-up

Props
Long black coat, sunglasses, notebook and pencil, powerful torch, £5 note, handwritten note or invoice, bell to make the sound of the phone (optional)

This is a retelling of the Unforgiving Servant parable. The two detectives, particularly Dexter, should be cool. Begin with the narrator standing alone on stage, stage left.

Narrator   Frisk and Dexter ran a time-travel investigation agency. They were detectives who could investigate any crime from any time. When the purple phone on Dexter's desk rang like an old school bell, they knew that a case from history was calling them. Dexter wore a long black coat and had a dog called Bilko.

(*Dexter walks on wearing a long black coat. He mimes pulling a dog on a lead.*)

Narrator Frisk wore small, dark glasses and always carried a notebook.

(*Frisk walks on putting on his dark glasses.*)

Narrator One day the purple phone rang.

(*Dexter mimes picking up a phone.*)

Narrator And Frisk and Dexter found themselves standing in a police station. Suddenly a man stepped in.

(*Derek enters, with his hands around his throat.*)

Derek Help! Help! Someone's just tried to kill me!

Narrator Frisk looked all around and spotted a nearby interview room.

(*Frisk looks all over then points dramatically.*)

Narrator They took the man inside to get the full story.

(*Dexter pulls a torch from his pocket and shines it in Derek's face, while Frisk makes notes.*)

Narrator The man was called Derek and he had been attacked while on his way to work. A man leapt out . . .

(*Derek leaps in the air, and beats himself up to demonstrate.*)

Narrator Grabbed him by the throat . . .

(*Derek grabs his own throat again.*)

Narrator And throttled him.

(*Derek throttles himself and falls over as if dead.*)

Dexter Hmm, what we need is a line-up.

(*Dexter rubs his chin and then snaps his fingers. Pete and the two extras shuffle into a line on stage. Dexter and Derek walk up and down the line-up. Frisk stands to one side.*)

Dexter Take your time.

(*Frisk looks fed up and sighs as he waits. Dexter and Derek continue walking up and down the line.*)

Derek   Him.

(*Derek points at Frisk. Frisk looks horrified, Dexter pulls Derek aside and whispers in his ear. Derek shrugs and walks up and down again. He stops suddenly and does a double take at Pete.*)

Derek   That's him!

(*Frisk and Dexter clap their hands on Pete's shoulders.*)

Dexter   What's all this about?

(*Pete points at Derek.*)

Pete   Okay, I admit I grabbed him, but he owes me £5.

Derek   Oh no I don't!

Pete   Oh yes you do!

Derek   Oh no I don't!

Narrator   It was all turning into a bit of a pantomime.

Pete   Oh no you don't!

Derek   Oh yes I do . . . Oop!

(*Derek claps a hand to his mouth.*)

Dexter   Aha! Gotcha! A confession!

Derek   Okay, I admit it, but I'm broke, I can't pay.

(*Dexter frisks Derek.*)

Narrator   They searched Derek and he was indeed broke.

Dexter   Fair enough.

(*Derek shakes his head and looks sad.*)

Pete   Fair enough? What d'you mean – fair enough?

Frisk   He hasn't got any money. You'll just have to let him off, Pete.

(*Pete shakes his head and stamps his foot stubbornly.*)

Pete   No way! He owes me!

(*Dexter starts frisking Pete.*)

Pete   Hey! What ya doing?

(*Dexter finds a piece of notepaper, he reads it quickly and shows it to Frisk who looks horrified.*)

Dexter   Looks like you owe someone some money yourself, Pete. In fact, looks like you owe somebody . . . 20,000 pounds!

(*Frisk faints and Dexter has to revive him by fanning his face with the note. Frisk grabs the note, gets up and points at it.*)

Frisk   But wait a minute – look! It says the debt's been cancelled. He doesn't have to pay! He's been let off.

Pete   They let me off, because I couldn't pay. I haven't got 20,000 pounds. I had to get on my knees and beg and beg and beg and beg . . .

(*Pete falls on his knees and hangs on to Dexter's trouser leg. Dexter looks embarrassed.*)

Dexter   Yes I think we've got the picture . . . Well Derek's broke too, and he only owes you a fiver – so you should let him off.

(*Pete stands up and mimes some angry muttering. He stomps up and down shaking his head and muttering.*)

Frisk   You've been let off a much bigger debt. So you really should let him off.

Narrator But the man wasn't too keen on that, so Frisk and Dexter locked him up for throttling Derek.

(*'Clang!' Frisk and Dexter and Derek, the throttled man, all say this together, and Pete mimes holding onto a barred window, facing the audience and looking at them sadly through the bars. Derek dusts his hands off and walks off, satisfied that justice has been done.*)

Narrator As Frisk and Dexter ran back to the future,

(*Frisk and Dexter run on the spot, side-on to the audience.*)

Narrator Frisk made a note of the case in his little black notebook. He said:

Frisk   Judging by this case I reckon it's better to forgive people and let them off a debt than hold a grudge and make them pay.

Narrator   And Dexter replied:

(*Dexter stops running and just pants very loudly, out of breath.*)

Narrator   The end.

(*Frisk and Dexter and the Narrator take a bow.*)

Mad Margaret, Reckless Rita and Shifty Sue

Bible reference
Mathew 25.14-30

Themes
The parable of the talents, using the gifts God has given us,
we all have gifts and talents we can use

Cast
Narrator
Mad Margaret
Reckless Rita
Shifty Sue
Mr Duff, the boss

Props
None

This is a group mime set in a café. The Narrator remains stage left throughout.
Begin with the Narrator and the three sisters on stage. As the piece begins Mad
Margaret mimes cooking, Reckless Rita mimes cleaning and Shifty Sue mimes
washing up, all in the café.

Narrator   Once upon a time there were three sisters. Mad Margaret,
Reckless Rita and Shifty Sue.

(They each step forward and wave, then step back, as their name is called.)
They all worked in a café with their boss Mr Duff.

(*Mr Duff walks on and waves to them.*)

> And one day Mr Duff went away for a holiday. Before he left he gave them all some money and told them to do something useful with it while he was gone.

(*Mr Duff mimes handing each of them a bag of money, one at a time.*)

> Mad Margaret was a really good cook so she went off, bought a whole trolley full of eggs, flour and milk and made 100 gallons of batter and started making delicious pancakes.

(*Mad Margaret snaps her fingers as if thinking of a good idea, then she starts breaking eggs into a bowl. She breaks hundreds of them, speeding up as she goes.*)

> When people smelt them they came to see her and she quickly sold all her pancakes and had to go and make some more.

(*Margaret mimes tossing pancakes while Rita and Sue mime handing out plates to imaginary customers.*)

> Meanwhile, Reckless Rita was really good at DIY, so she went off to B&Q and bought lots of paint and shelves and screws.

(*Margaret and Sue freeze while Rita snaps her fingers and mimes picking up a tin of paint and a brush.*)

> And while Margaret was making pancakes she gave the whole place a complete makeover, and when people saw the new sign and the new shop front they came to see what was going on.

(*Rita starts painting and Sue and Margaret come to life and admire the walls around them and nod.*)

> Then they smelt the pancakes and bought lots of them.

(*Margaret tosses pancakes again and Sue hands out plates while Rita continues painting.*)

> Meanwhile, Shifty Sue was really good at writing, so she went out and bought some nice pens and some coloured card to make brand new menus . . .

(*Sue mimes cutting card with some scissors.*)

But then,

(*Sue pauses, yawns and shakes her head.*)

She got bored, changed her mind, and took them back to the shop.

(*Sue picks up a pile of card and pens and throws them off-stage.*)

Then she put her money back in the sack, which she hid amongst the huge pile of empty egg cartons and paint pots at the back of the café.

(*Sue mimes hiding the bag at the back of the stage, behind Margaret and Rita.*)

Then she fell asleep.

(*She yawns and lies down on the stage and goes to sleep.*)

As soon as Mr Duff came back in through the door Margaret said, 'Have a pancake!'

(*Margaret holds out a plate as Mr Duff walks back on.*)

Rita said, 'Mind the wet paint!'

(*Rita grabs him and pulls him away from some imaginary wet patch and dusts him down.*)

And Sue woke up and said, 'Here's your money back, all safe and sound'.

(*Sue wakes, sees what's going on, digs around for her bag and runs to Mr Duff with it.*)

Mr Duff took one look inside the bag and said, 'I didn't want it back, I wanted you to do something useful with it'.

(*Mr Duff takes the bag, looks inside and looks horrified.*)

'Oh!' said Sue.

(*Sue claps a hand across her open mouth.*)

Then, while Mr Duff sat and ate a pancake with extra chocolate sauce, he admired the new paint and wallpaper.

(*Mr Duff mimes sitting down and eating, while looking around and nodding happily; Margaret, Rita and Sue queue up next to him.*)

Then he gave Margaret a pay rise . . .

(*Mr Duff mimes giving Margaret some money, she takes it and walks round him.*)

He gave Rita a pay rise . . .

(*Mr Duff mimes giving Rita some money, she takes it and walks round him.*)

And he gave Sue . . .

(*Sue holds out her hand for her pay rise. Mr Duff just looks at her empty hand.*)

The sack.

(*Mr Duff points off-stage. Sue looks horrifed then turns and walks off stage.*)

Oh dear.

(*Margaret and Rita shake their heads sadly. They all look at the audience and freeze.*)

Wise and foolish

Bible reference
Luke 6.47-49

Themes
The parable of the wise and foolish men;

Cast
1
2
3
4

Props
Whistle, two pairs of gloves, two bow ties,
two hats (one smart for the wise man, the other silly)

This is a piece of physical theatre, i.e. lively, loud and energetic. It moves along at a good pace and quickly switches from one picture or scene to another. Begin with four people in a line, standing with their backs to the audience as below:
1 2 3 4

(2 blows a whistle and 3 jumps round and says:)

3   Here's a story, a story for you,

         'Bout a fool and a wise man too.

         Jesus says:

(All jump round, pointing finger and say, 'Which one are you?')

3   Wise or foolish, I'm asking you.

(1 steps forward and says:)

1 I am the wise man. Got it all right.

Gonna build me a house, gonna make it right!

(*1 freezes. 4 steps forward and says:*)

4 Then I must be the foolish one.

Gonna build me a house as fast as I can!

(*Both repeat their lines together three times, putting on gloves, bow ties and hats while they speak. They then freeze. 2 and 3 step forward, right index finger raised, and say, in rhythm:*)

2, 3 Right – we need – to build – a house!

(*All say this four more times, looking high and low as they do so. The last time through 1 cuts in and shouts 'THERE!' and points stage right. He then takes three steps in that direction saying: 'Mm. Mm. Mmm!' (one 'Mm' on each step).*)

(*All then clap their hands twice and say 'Here', and point to the spot that the wise man is on. The foolish man claps but points in the wrong direction.*)

1 Right, let's get going . . . we'll have a coffee break in a minute, bring that digger over here . . . right let's have some work done.

(*1 shouts this and 2 and 3 join him and mime working with the appropriate noises. 4 steps over to them and jumps in front – they stop dead. 4 knocks on the ground several times, then kicks it with his foot.*)

4 Ow! Look what that's done to my . . . ooh!

(*Before 4 can finish he is scooped up into the arms of 2, 1 then moves round and holds 4's feet, so that 4 is now carried by 1 and 2.*)

4 Rock! Man, that's solid!

Others Oh yeah!

4 Too solid.

(*1, 2 and 3 now take three steps sideways towards stage left, still carrying 4, who is draped in their arms. They step as they say 'What I need'.*)

1, 2, 3 What I need

4 Is soft.

1,2,3 What I need

4	Is easy.
1, 2, 3	What I need
4	Is sand!

(*1, 2 and 3 look down in horror at the ground and say, 'Sand!'*)

3	You can't build on that!
1 and 2	It's too soft!
4	Shut up! My house – my decision.

(*1 and 2 look at each other and drop 4. 1 marches back to his building site. 1 mimes drilling with appropriate noise, 4 mimes using a bucket and spade for a few seconds, builds then shouts, 'FINISHED'.*)

(*1 and 4 freeze, apart from beating out a rhythm for 2 and 3. 2 and 3 step centre stage. 3 becomes a weather map, 2 the weather man. 2 takes 3's arm as a pointer, and says, in time with the rhythm:*)

2   There'll be . . .

Rain in the north (*Points up*)

And hail, in the south. (*Points down*)

Floods in the mouth of the estuary. (*Points at 3's open mouth*)

From 'ere and 'ere (*Points at both ears*)

There'll be snow and sleet,

At least two feet of water. (*Points at feet*)

Wind (*Points at mouth*) and gales, rain and hail,

The whole outlook looks bad. (*Stop rhythm at this point.*)

In summary – the pits. (*Lifts 3's arm and points at 3's armpit.*)

(*3 then places a hand on 2's head, pushes 2 down and points at 1, saying:*)

3	Meanwhile, back at the building site . . .
1	Finished.

(*All look up, hold out a hand for rain and say, 'Oh, oh!' They then all make storm sounds, and 1 and 4 are swept around the stage, colliding twice. The first time they collide 1 pulls 4's hat over his eyes and pushes him away, the second time 4 grabs 1's leg for safety and 1 looks embarrassed and brushes 4 away, saying:)*

1   Get off my leg!

(All freeze after this, then 2 and 3 step forward holding cups of water. They tap 1 and 4 on the shoulder. As they turn round 2 and 3 throw the water in their faces! Then they grab 1 and 4 and pull them around on the spot shouting:)

2, 3   Wind and gales, rain and hail! *(three times)*

(After the third time 4 is thrown to the ground by 3, and 1 and 2 look at him in horror. 4 crawls on knees scrabbling at the ground.)

4   My house – it's gone!

(4 then takes three soggy steps over to 1. The others make three squelching sounds as he steps. 4 says to 1:)   *-*

4   My house fell down!

(1 claps hands in front of 4's face. 4 falls back into 2's arms.)

1   Should've built on rock then . . .

3   Not sand!

1   Should've built on rock then . . .

3   Not sand!

(4 claps hands twice, then twice again. All turn and point at audience and say:)

1, 2, 3, 4 It's the same with Jesus Christ, he can help you live your life – listen to him or you might sink!

(2 blows whistle twice. On the second blast 1, 3 and 4 all flop over. All freeze.)

Specks and logs

Bible reference
Matthew 7.1-5

Themes
Don't judge other people when you have the same problems and faults, don't be hypocritical

Cast
Narrator

Wife

Husband

Props
Large story book

Tie with a few small coloured stains on it

Jacket with huge brown stains all over the back

Begin with the Narrator on stage, holding a large story book. After the Narrator's introduction, the Narrator can leave, or step back and watch the action in the background, stage left. However if they do this they must remain still so as not to distract from the action on stage.

Narrator   Jesus told lots of stories. They were fun to listen to, but they also made people think about life, and sometimes he surprised them at the end. Like the time he told a story about a man who had a tiny speck of dust in his eye, and he got told off about it by another man who had a whole tree in his eye! That's a strange story isn't it? I know, let's look at it a different way. Imagine a husband and wife getting ready to go out for the evening.

(*A husband and wife walk on, they are preparing for an evening out. He helps her on with her jacket, being careful not to allow the audience to see the back of the jacket. She notices a few stains on his tie.*)

Wife   (*Impatiently*) Oh look, how on earth did you manage that?

Husband I just slipped, that's all.

Wife   But red wine, I ask you.

Husband It's rosé actually.

Wife   Oh the good stuff, what a waste.

Husband (*Pulls out a handkerchief*) Listen don't make such a fuss, it's only a few spots.

Wife   But it's your best tie.

Husband Yes, but it is getting old, and I never did like it that much.

Wife   I bought you that tie.

Husband Oh! Did you? Well, it'll be all right, there's no need to keep on.

Wife   But we're going to my mother's, what on earth will she think?

Husband (*Astonished*) Think! I didn't know your mother ever did . . .

Wife   I'll ignore that comment. What are you going to do about this mess?

Husband It's not a mess.

Wife   It is. You look terrible, it's all over the place.

Husband You're exaggerating as usual.

Wife   Oh am I? Well, I'll tell you one thing. I'm not going out with you while you look like that. You're just an embarrassment to me. Now give me that cloth . . .

(*The wife turns to wipe off the stains, revealing a much larger stain down the back of her jacket. Both freeze.*)

Invitation to dinner

Bible reference
Matthew 22.1-14

Themes
The parable of the banquet, many people are invited to come but
many don't want to

Cast
Eddie, the Narrator
King Size, the king and Eddie's boss
King's friend
King's brother-in-law
Two servants, who later become the guests at the banquet

Props
Suitcase, cape and crown, table, party hats, paper plates,
and other party accessories

*Enter Eddie, a cool cockney, in shades and leather jacket, and carrying a suitcase
labelled 'Ed Case'. He sets the case down and addresses the audience.*

Eddie   Hi, my name's Eddie, and this 'ere (*Indicates with his
                 thumb*) is my boss – King Size.

(*Enter King Size, looking regal and pompous, dressed in a cape and crown. He
strides to centre stage and stands regally surveying the audience. Eddie sniffs and
continues.*)

Eddie   Just now, 'e's decided to throw a party.

(*Enter the two servants, carrying a table. They chat among themselves in rough
and ready fashion about football and the lottery and other such trivial matters.*

They hustle the King out of the way so that they can put the table down centre stage.)

Servant   Mind out guv.

(They disappear off-stage and return carrying a chair each and a few party hats. All the time the King is made to feel in the way and Eddie watches from a safe distance, stage right. They pile stuff on the King, and eventually push him down onto one of the chairs.)

Servant   Have a seat guv, you're making the place look untidy.

(These preparations continue, the servants carrying on more and more stuff and piling it on the King.)

Eddie   So, as I said 'e's throwing a party, or p'raps I should say, the party's being thrown at him.

(At this point one of the servants throws a packet of balloons at the King – they hit him in the chest and he clutches them hastily.)

Eddie   Anyway, my boss likes big parties.

(They throw the King a party hat.)

Eddie   In fact – the bigger the better.

(They throw him a huge party hat.)

Eddie   So, when everything was ready . . .

(The servants take no notice and continue chatting and moving stuff around.)

Eddie   Ahem, when everything was ready . . .

(Still they take no notice.)

Eddie   *(Shouts)* WHEN EVERYTHING WAS READY!

(The servants realize and make a hasty exit, leaving the King on the stage in the midst of the chaos.)

Eddie   Well, when everything was as ready as it could be . . . my boss decides to call up his mates.

King   I think I'll call my friends.

Eddie   Good idea mush. So he gets on the blower like and rings 'em all up. But do they wanna know? Do they Bob Monkhouse! No way!

(The King mimes a telephone conversation, suddenly becoming angry as he listens to the reply at the other end.)

Eddie   So my boss, who's a stubborn lot, puts his foot down,

(King stamps his foot, crushing his party hat underneath it.)

Eddie   With a firm hand.

(King bashes his fist on the table, knocking things onto the floor and hurting his hand.)

Eddie   He rolls up his sleeves, flexes his muscles,

(King does this, then hurts his arm while flexing his muscles.)

Eddie   Plucks up all his courage . . . and sends me out to do his dirty work.

(King boldly snaps his fingers at Eddie and points off stage.)

Eddie   So off I goes to see why these diamond geezers ain't comin' to my old man's do.

(Eddie opens his case and pulls out a huge truncheon or baseball bat.)

Eddie   So there I am, innocently walking along,

(He patrols the front of the stage, truncheon in hand, eyeing the audience suspiciously.)

Eddie   When who should I happen to bump off . . . Er I mean bump into, but my boss's best mate.

(Enter King Size's best friend, innocently strolling along. Eddie pounces on him, grabs him by the throat and threatens him with the truncheon.)

Eddie   Why ain't you comin' to my boss's do?

Friend   Well I'd love to . . .

Eddie   Good, well that's settled then.

(Eddie lets him go, thinking he has consented to come.)

Friend   But I've got this awful leak in the kitchen roof . . .

(He is splashed with water from off-stage.)

Friend   As you can see . . .

(He hurries off while he has the chance.)

Eddie   He'll have a leak somewhere else in a minute . . . Oh well, I guess he was a bit of a drip anyway.

(*Eddie shrugs and turns back to audience.*)

Eddie   Next, who should I run into . . .

(*Eddie turns side on just as King Size's brother-in-law enters stage left and runs straight into Eddie. Eddie grabs him by the collar and turns to the audience with an evil grin.*)

Eddie   The boss's brother-in-law! Well? Why ain't you comin' to my boss's party?

Brother-in-law (*Struggling for words and gasping for breath*) Erm, well I . . . well I . . . well I . . .

Eddie   Yeah, I got that bit already. What else?

Brother-in-law Really . . . I'd dearly . . . love to . . .

Eddie   Oh well, that's settled then.

(*Eddie starts to drag him off to the King.*)

Brother-in-law But, but . . . my wife! She's expecting a baby any minute! Imminently!

Eddie   My boss is expecting a party – imminently!

Brother-in-law Sorry! Must dash!

(*Brother-in-law makes a hasty and relieved exit, wiping his brow as he goes.*)

Eddie   Hang on! You ain't married! Oh, drat! (*Turns back to audience*) So off he trots. I dunno, talk about lame excuses, he *is* a lame excuse. Anyway this caper goes on all afternoon, and all I come up with is a load of hard luck stories, and more important – no punters for the party. So, 'ere's me. Sore feet, sore 'ead and sore afraid of what the boss's gonna say when I get home.

King   What! No one?

(*Eddie throws himself at the King's feet and grovels there.*)

Eddie   Sorry, guv, they would have come – if it was at all humanly possible, it's just . . . they didn't wanna. (*To audience*) I knew he'd be extremely angry.

King	I'm extremely angry.

Eddie   What did I tell you? So there's me, expecting the boss to explode any minute, but does he? Does he Bob Monkhouse! No way. For once he keeps his head, and his party. And this time he flexes his muscles, tones up his biceps, combs his hair, touches up his make-up (*The King does all these in quick succession as Eddie says them*), oils his knees, does a few press ups – and pulls a ligament. So guess who gets to do the 'ard graft again? Yeah. Muggins 'ere. (*He taps his chest.*)

(*The King calls him over and whispers loudly and incomprehensibly in Eddie's ear.*)

King   Shubadubwubadubshubashubadoobawobbaslobba (*etc.*)

Eddie   But this time 'e sends me out to bring in all the beggars off the street and the poor geezers who ain't got enough money, 'cause them toffs he invited first don't deserve to come, so now 'e's inviting those who *will* come. Those who wanna. And *this* time I gets to pick 'em up in the gaffer's best Rolls, even though I went and crashed it only last month.

(*The King has second thoughts and waves Eddie back again.*)

King   Shubadubwubadubshubashubadoobawobbaslobba (*etc.*)

Eddie   Oh! Right. Well, ahem, actually he's lettin' me have his Skoda instead, but it's still better than leggin' it. Right? Anyway, to cut a long story short, I got all these punters in for the party.

(*He whistles at the folks off stage.*)

Eddie   Oi!

(*The servants come in, dressed now in dirty old jackets as guests with glasses in their hands.*)

Eddie   And the place was packed out, I can tell you. And there we all are 'avin' a right old knees-up, when who should stroll in, but the boss's brother-in-law. And as you can guess, the boss was mighty pleased to see him.

(*The brother-in-law strolls nonchalantly in, glass in hand, he looks at the other guests, sniffs and turns his nose up at them. The King rushes over and grabs him by the scruff of the neck.*)

Eddie   Especially as he'd slipped in without a ticket. And after turning down a personal invite. So, my boss, being a considerate man like, seeing as his brother-in-law was obviously a bit shy about visiting his imaginary wife and new baby, thought he'd better give him a bit of an incentive to go down the hospital, i.e. two broken arms and a broken leg.

(*The King and the other two guests physically evict the brother-in-law, who is mouthing protests.*)

Eddie   Now this 'ere's only a story of course, but it's very important, 'cause it's a story that Jesus told about the kingdom of God. You see, God's like our real boss, and he's throwing a party for everyone, and he sent his son Jesus along to tell us about it. But it's up to us. We don't have to go, we can think of a few excuses and pretend we don't wanna. But just remember, there's no gatecrashin' once the party starts, if you ain't got a ticket, you'll be sent packin'.

(*He picks up his case and pats it as he says this last line. Then he grins at the audience and taps the side of his nose knowingly.*)

Eddie   See ya round!

(*Eddie turns smartly and struts off stage. The others follow.*)

Church life

A history lesson

Bible reference

A swift overview of the Old Testament and the Gospel story

Themes

The Bible, Creation through to the coming of Jesus

Cast

Narrator

Group of four to eight people

Props

None

The Narrator reads his/her lines whilst the group people act out the directions beneath. The group should freeze each position while the Narrator delivers each line.

Narrator   Looking back

(All turn and look behind.)

Down the history of the years many things come to mind

(The group look as if they can't think of anything.)

Don't they?

(All shake head helplessly.)

(Sighs heavily) All right, let's go back to the beginning . . . First – the big bang

(One of the group bursts a balloon, they all jump, including the Narrator.)

Or, perhaps we should say . . . Creation;

(All become builders/decorators/workmen saying phrases like 'Okay let's have this over here'; 'More light over there'; 'This star could do with another coat of paint'. They dig, paint, build, whistle,, etc.)

   Closely followed by the flood.

(One produces a water pistol and squirts 'rain' on others who make animal sounds.)

   Enter the children of Israel

(All become children, fighting, arguing.)

   And Moses – the leader;

(One shouts 'Quiet' to all the others who stop.)

   Joshua – the warrior;

(All adopt Kung Fu positions and shout 'Huh'.)

   And David – the king,

(All bow.)

   The poet

(All begin to say, 'There was a young man from (name of home town) . . .' limerick style.)

   And the lead guitarist.

(All mime playing electric guitars and head banging.)

   After that it all went downhill

(All look down, stage left.)

   'Till God sent Jesus

(One says 'Look' and all look stage right.)

   Who loved people,

(All shout 'Yo!' and slap hands and laugh.)

   Parties,

(All hold sherry glasses and look polite.)

   Stories,

(All say, 'Did you hear the one about . . .'.)

And sinners.

(*Adopt different sinful poses.*)

But he didn't like hypocrites much

(*Look pious and sing, 'A-a-amen'.*)

And they didn't like him,

(*Shout 'NO!'*)

So they put him somewhere for safekeeping . . .

(*They crucify one of the group and then gather round him/her and push him/her to the floor.*)

But Jesus was irrepressible. You can't keep a good man down!

(*Look amazed, say 'He's back!' as the figure leaps up into the air, very much alive.*)

And down through the ages

(*Mime opening an old dusty book.*)

He has changed and inspired men and women all over the world;

(*Adopt different poses of life – walking, talking, typing, running, digging, sleeping, laughing, crying, etc.*)

And what began 2000 years ago with one man called Jesus in Israel is now all over the place, in America, Africa, Europe, Asia, China, India, Antarctica, Basingstoke . . .

(*All look and point in different directions.*)

And down through the ages millions and millions of people who once felt that they were nothing

(*Look sad and downtrodden, fed up and poor.*)

Discovered that they were actually very important

(*One of group opens the book again and shouts 'WOW!' Others gather round them.*)

To God.

(*Look up, shocked, and freeze in that position.*)

Dirk Digweed
and Derek Doodle

Bible reference
1 Corinthians 12

Themes
God gives us all different and special gifts to do the jobs
he wants us to do, Pentecost

Cast
Two narrators, 1 and 2
Dirk Digweed
Derek Doodle

Props
All mimed, so do practise them carefully

Enter two narrators, 1 and 2. They stand stage right and left. The narration should be presented with life and vigour, not merely read.

1   Hello.

2   We'd like to tell you a story.

1   In fact – this is that well known parable –

2   'The Drama of

1   Dirk Digweed

2   And Derek Doodle'.

1   (*Checking the script*) Dirk Digweed?

2   Yes.

1   And Derek Doodle?

2   That's the one.

1   Never heard of it.

2   (*Warming to the task*) Oh well, in that case . . . One day it was Dirk Digweed's birthday.

(*Dirk and Derek enter, Dirk smiling proudly. Derek offers him a cake (this is mimed). Dirk counts the candles, takes a deep breath and blows. 2 makes a rather noisy 'blowing out candles' sound.*)

(*Derek carefully wipes his eye after Dirk has blown, then mimes singing the second half of 'Happy Birthday'.*)

1   (*Out of tune*) 'Happy Birthday dear Dirk, Happy Birthday to you'.

2   And for his birthday

1   Dirk received a variety of gifts.

(*Dirk mimes picking up a small box and then unwraps it. Derek watches enviously, peering over Dirk's shoulder. Dirk puts his fingers into the tiny box and pulls out a long umbrella. Derek and the narrators are amazed! Dirk puts the umbrella up, and as he leans back to look up for the rain he pokes Derek in the eye with the end of it.*)

2   Some of them useful.

1   Some . . . not so useful.

(*Dirk picks up another object. Looks at it, shrugs, turns it round, offers it to Derek, who refuses it. Eventually he looks round awkwardly and slings it over his shoulder.*)

2   But from Derek he received: 'Derek Doodle's Deluxe Do-it-yourself Directory!'

(*Derek bashfully produces his present from behind his back. It is a very large book. Dirk is over the moon and excitedly rips off the wrapping paper and thumbs through it.*)

1   Because . . . Derek wanted Dirk

2   To build him something!

1   Dirk was over the moon and quickly decided to build Derek a huge swimming pool.

(*Dirk points to the page he has found. Derek is horrified.*)

2   With a sauna. (*Dirk fans himself.*)

1   A multiple diving board . . . Boiing! (*Dirk dives happily.*)

2   Water skiing facilities . . . Rrrm rrrm! (*Dirk starts up an outboard motor.*)

1   And changing rooms.

(*Dirk turns his back on the audience and bashfully mimes changing.*)

2   All in Derek's back garden.

(*They both lean on a fence and stare into the back garden.*)

1   Which was two foot by six.

2   An ambitious project,

1   In fact, so ambitious

(*Dirk begins to have doubts.*)

2   That Dirk gave up the idea because Derek only wanted him to make a kennel in the first place.

1   Woof! Woof!

(*Derek patiently flips through the book and shows Dirk the correct page, then he picks up a box of tools and offers it to Dirk.*)

2   Derek said:

1   'Here, you'll need some tools'.

(*Derek taps Dirk's shoulder. Dirk is engrossed in the book.*)

2   Dirk said:

1   'Don't bother me now, Derek, I've got a job to do'.

2   So he set to work.

(*Derek shrugs and leaves. Dirk mimes carrying on a floor, roof and walls.*)

1   With a floor,

2 A roof,

1 And . . . *five* walls?

(*Dirk is confused.*)

2 Maths wasn't Dirk's strong point.

1 But improvising was . . .

(*Dirk hastily throws the items together at top speed.*)

2 And soon

1 He'd finished.

(*Dirk proudly leans on the kennel.*)

2 It was a fine, strong, sturdy kennel

1 That quickly collapsed.

(*Dirk falls over as the kennel suddenly collapses.*)

2 What you might call

1 A 'collapsible' kennel.

2 Oh dear.

1 The problem was that Dirk didn't possess a screwdriver . . . or a hammer . . . or a monkey wrench. Not even a bent nail.

2 Enter Derek. (*Derek enters and waves happily.*)

1 'Hi, Dirk!'

2 Said Derek.

1 'How's it all going? Need anything?'

2 (*Angrily*) 'Monkey wrench!'

1 'Same to you!'

2 'NO! I need one!'

1 Dirk shouted.

2 'It was a stupid idea of yours – getting me to build a kennel when you know I don't have the right tools. What sort of a friend are you? You're just a right silly saus . . .

1 (*Hastily cutting in*) Derek waved his box of tools at Dirk.

2   Which was no mean feat because it weighed a ton!

(*Derek's arm drops suddenly.*)

1   'I had the tools all the time!' said Derek.

2   'Then why didn't you give them to me?'

1   'I tried to. But you were so engrossed in your own ideas . . .'

(*Dirk listens to this and looks sheepish.*)

2   Dirk was sorry.

1   'Sorry.'

2   Said Dirk.

1   'Oh, that's okay. Just remember to ask for them next time, you can't do a job without the right equipment.'

(*Derek hands the box to Dirk.*)

2   'Next time?'

1   'Oh yes, I forgot to mention – when you've finished the kennel I'd like a swimming pool!'

2   'What!'

1   Said Dirk.

(*Dirk freezes for a moment, looking horrified, then he accidentally drops the box on Derek's foot.*)

2   'Ow!'

1   Said Derek.

(*This is an extreme understatement as Derek is in absolute agony, he mimes cussing and swearing and hobbles painfully off. Dirk looks at the audience and shrugs. All freeze.*)

Worship

Bible reference

Romans 12.1

Themes

Worship in our everyday lives, living as a Christian

Cast

Narrator

Group of four to eight people who illustrate the narrative

Props

None

Worship is so often seen as a Sunday morning engagement, but it is much more than that. It is a daily activity, and should be reflected in every part of our lives. This is a simple sketch that seeks to illustrate that. The group stand in a straight line with the Narrator at one end.

Narrator Worship

(All clap once.)

What is it?

(All shrug.)

It's love

(Group freeze in positions of helping one another.)

Reaching out, reaching up.

(All look up sharply, still in pose.)

It's life-style

Curtain Up

(*Adopt different poses: sleep, read, phone, type, chat.*)
> In work, or at play – home and away.

> Worship

(*Clap.*)
> What is it?

(*Shrug.*)
> It's giving: being generous

(*Reach in pockets.*)
> And quick to serve.

(*Wash feet in pairs.*)
> It's praise – reaching out

(*Sing, pray, read, worship.*)
> Reaching up.

(*Again, look up sharply, still in positions.*)
> On our lips

(*Open mouth, as if to speak.*)
> And in our lives.

(*Shake hands.*)

> Worship

(*Clap.*)
> What is it?

(*Shrug.*)
> It's a celebration.

(*All rejoice.*)
> God's love touching our lives.